Author's Note

This book existed only in my list of good intentions and wishes for the future. This manuscript wandered like a leaf falling through the air of my thoughts. However, my loyal conscience never stopped repeating… *"Jesus has done many things for you! What have you done for Him?"*

The fact is that I met Jesus Christ in person many years ago, but I kept my silence. So, I wrote this collection of memories because of a feeling of remorse. But by all means, always hoping that it will help someone, somehow, someday. And this is the story…

This book is a Christian testimony and partly an autobiography. All the human characters depicted in this story in the countries of USA and Mexico are real-life characters.

Written & author's picture by Virgo Zusa
Xavier and Theresa Rodriguez's picture by J.R.
Consultant for English language by www.fiverr.com/bluston
Proofread for English by www.fiverr.com/pencilprincess7
Main cover design by www.fiverr.com/jeweldesign
Mock cover design on page 7 by Virgo Zusa
Mock cover design on page 45 by www.fiverr.com/dickyjdesign
Mock cover design on page 69, 151 by www. fiverr.com/vicovers
Mock cover design on page 168 by www.fiverr.com/muradezizov

ISBN-10: 0-692-79756-4
ISBN-13: 978-0-692-79756-3

Printed in USA
Edition edited on January 2021

For Roman

Dear youngest brother, this is my testimony. I hope that you will write yours soon. Never let yourself be defeated by evil.

INDEX

ACKNOWLEDGMENTS AND DEDICATION

To start, I want to express my gratitude and dedicate this book to Jesus Christ. The God who became a mortal man and walked among us in flesh and bone, just as any other human being. He was condemned to death, but he resurrected on the third day. I have seen him in person, and I know that he is well and that he lives and reigns forever in the fullness of glory. Without his forgiveness and his help, I would never have been able to tell this story. Next, I want to thank my parents for the love they have always had for their children – no matter how bad we, their children, have behaved so many times. Similarly, I thank my brother in Christ, *Xavier Rodriguez,* for God used him to set me free and to give me a new life. Likewise, I also thank my relatives and friends who read this book before it was published, and encouraged me to continue by giving me all sorts of corrections and constructive criticism – in addition to allowing me to use their real names in this tale.

I take this opportunity to apologize to the persons I mobbed, robbed, mistreated, lied to, mocked, and offended. I am letting you all know that I have been punished for that already. I am trying to be a better human being each day of my life, and I will continue striving as long as God allows me to continue living on this world.

INTRODUCTION

Dear reader, I have two pieces of big news that I need to give you. The first piece of news is not so good, but the second one is excellent. First, I will start with the bad news. I have to tell you that the place called *Hell* is real. I did spend some time in the gates of Hell, for this reason I bear witness to the fact that it does exist, and I will talk more about that in a later chapter of this book. The good news is that the place called *Heaven* also exists, and that... Jesus Christ is also real! I had a personal encounter with him. This book is a Christian testimony and partly an autobiography. To summarize the story I tell here, I will say that as a child I challenged Satan, and this fact caused me infinite problems. Later, as I grew in age, I came to consider myself as a person who would live and die without never being able to knowing God. The concept of God and Satan became for me a fantasy tale, a fable for children.

Although, everything changed when one day a relative of mine had a problem, and while trying to help my family member, I sought God's help as I had never done it before in my life. The marvelous thing is that God responded, and it was then that I had a personal encounter with Jesus of Nazareth.

In the next pages, I will give you **<<four>>** steps to follow, so that you too can have an encounter with Jesus, and in the process ensure the salvation of your soul as well. Those four steps were shown to me by divine providence and I know that they will be as great a help for you as they were for me. Along with that, it will be good for you to know that the salvation of the soul – is neither a philosophy nor a fairy tale. Being saved is a unique and a personal experience. Yes, you read that right. I have said that the salvation of your soul is something that you really can experience. Salvation is neither a *maybe* nor a *perhaps,* but instead is a complete conviction that you are saved.

Dear reader, let me ask you a question, and please be honest in answering it. If you were to die at this very moment, would you go to heaven? If your answer is – I do not know, perhaps, probably, or I am definitely not going to heaven – then I must tell you that this book has been written especially for you.

The experience of the salvation of your soul is a **one hundred-percent** absolute trust that Jesus has saved you because you know it, and because you can feel it too.

Perhaps you may find it strange that in this moment I am telling you that this book is not just one more written work about religion. What happens is that I consider religion **<<greatly>>** responsible for driving humans away from God.

One day I realized that religion imposes hard burdens on humans, and that these burdens are sometimes even impossible to keep up with and to follow. In consequence, this has made the religious person to conform to learn moral laws that are more useful in the social, and cultural realm, than in the spiritual domain. This may create in the individual – a certain satisfaction of conscience – meaning that by merely attending Sunday's mass, **<<peace>>** has already been achieved with the Creator of the Heavens.

Dear reader, I let you know that if you are one of the people who acts that way, unfortunately you are living in a lie. That is because such standards of human behavior, in the end, fall short of showing the individual the actual path to eternal life. Although, I hope that by reading this book and by making a personal decision, you will not **<<perish>>** in such a falsehood.

If we can remember, the Bible recounts in the book of Genesis chapter three, that God himself used to come to Earth to talk to Adam and Eve, and he used to do this – *face to face*. From there we can see that the Almighty Lord, seeks and desires a personal relationship with human beings. Even though such fellowship was destroyed by the sin and the disobedience of men. Despite all that, the Father of Mercy, willing to continue with a personal relationship with the human race – *envisioned a plan*.

Now the sin and disobedience of man are forgiven through Jesus Christ, who has become the door or the bridge, to a new personal and intimate relationship between humanity and the All-knowing Father.

The first purpose of this book is to help the reader to become a spiritual individual. The second aim of this work is to help the reader to establish a real spiritual connection with God. By reaching these two objectives, the person will finally and triumphantly, leave the religiousness of this world in the past.

At the same time, I want to make it very clear that by writing this story, it has never been my intention to add a new doctrine to the Christian doctrine. But rather, what I am looking for is to explain about the four set of steps that my own life took to meet Jesus the Jewish Messiah. It is my complete belief that if you follow and perform the teachings written about in this book, you will also have a personal encounter with God, and a **<<legitimate>>** spiritual relationship with him. The steps to follow to save your soul are clear, they are simple, and easy to accomplish. In addition, I will also quote chapters and Bible verses to back up what I say. Dear reader, it is better to have the salvation of your soul and have no need for it, than to need it and not have it at the moment of your death – the instant when you leave this earthly physical world.

You have nothing to lose and everything to gain by following the advice that I will provide in these brief few pages. I will also add that the things you are about to read next, are not things I read in a book, or saw in a movie. This book is based on the true story of my own life and of my family's lives, and I bear witness that the things I have written are real, and are my truth. Everything is just as I have remembered, seen, felt, understood, heard, and lived it – although my tale may sound fantastic at times.

CHAPTER 1

BORN

THE STRANGE FOREST

I was in a strange forest. The woodland seemed very ancient, as each of the tree trunks had quite large dimensions. The outline of each tree was so enormous that it might have taken from eight to nine people holding hands together to encircle the circumference of a single tree. It is known that the thickness of a tree increases with age, and those trees looked as if they were hundreds of thousands of years old.

In front of me, and about six feet away, there was a young woman who looked to be around twenty-five years old. She had white skin and red hair that was straight and long, falling to her waist. Tied around her temples there was a thin band of dark brown leather that held and kept her hair away from her forehead and from her eyes.

The woman was tall, somewhere around 5.80 feet in height and had an overly athletic appearance. It was as if she was used to a daily life of a demanding and exhausting physical exercise.

All of her clothes were made of animal skin, and the skin displayed fur of a fiery reddish color just like the hue of a sunrise.

Her garments were short and comfortable enough to allow her to run, and to make any speedy movements without impediment.

That very same scanty costume also allowed me to see the entirety of her arms and of her legs. Her arms showed some well-defined and outlined muscles, but they did not lose their femininity. Her thighs showed a greater outline (because of muscle hypertrophy), because they were more pronounced than the muscles of her arms.

A man leaned on the right shoulder of that woman. The man also had a youthful appearance, but his hair was black. Like her, he also wore animal skins, but his entire outfit was a discolored, faded gray.

The young man appeared to have been wounded, and he was in a semi-unconscious state.

Now I was standing in front of them, and about eight steps away, and at that moment, my breathing was deep, and panting. I felt like if I was having a very hard time filling my lungs with air.

My mind reminded me of the past scenes of a mortal fight. Recent memories raced in my head that we had just escaped the ferocious attack of some primitive creatures that resembled ape-men, and they had chased us for a long stretch all throughout the forest. The appearance of these beings was as follows…

Mainly, these beings walked upright on two legs (*they were bipedal*). Moreover, I saw more than one of them repeatedly run semi-curved and touching the ground with the palms of their hands while doing it. Their faces looked like a combination of an ape's and a human being's, and they were completely covered with a short black fur, just like a chimpanzee. The strength of each one of them was colossal, far beyond the strength of a normal man. The average height of these ape-men was about 4.90 feet.

This primitive group of savages wanted to capture us, kill us, and what is most probably… Eat us. They were on a hunting campaign and for a moment we seemed to be the main dish of their menu of that day.

Luckily, their hunting weapons were much more rudimentary than the ones I was carrying with me. They hunted with long wooden sticks and sharp bones. But I also saw a couple of them throwing blow darts at me with a hollowed piece of bamboo that they were putting in their mouths. Possibly, those were poisoned or paralyzing darts.

I, instead, had a long and curved sword in my right hand. A dagger strapped to the forearm of my left arm, and another spare knife was firmly fastened to the thigh of my right leg.

What is more, all of my weapons were lethally sharp, and all were made of solid metal.

Therefore, my weapons gave me a considerable advantage against the primitive group of hunters. The hunting clan of the ape-men was made up of about thirty to thirty-five creatures. I defended my companions as best as I could, and apparently, with enough success. Since I had caused the ape-men so many casualties, that they had already given up on following us several minutes ago.

I knew exactly where I was located. In my mind, I had the map to reach the nearest civilized village to seek help for the young man who was almost passed out, and also to cure my wounds. Nevertheless, something was happening to me. My vision blurred and I could hardly breathe. I do not know if this was related to the fierce fight against the group of savage creatures. Maybe, I had not recuperated from the physical exhaustion I had suffered from the battle, and I had not recovered my breath (*because of the hyperventilation*). Or, it could have been because the multiple wounds I had received throughout the fight were starting to take a toll on my body. The auburn-haired woman knew that something was wrong with me. She opened her eyes very wide as if trying to understand what was happening to me, and she looked me in the face with a lot of attention, but did not say a word. I could see that her face showed shock and concern. The good thing is that she had no visible injuries, and that made me feel a little better.

Quite possibly, the ape-men wanted to capture her alive, and that was the reason why she seemed to be completely unharmed. However, I started to fall into a dreadful sleep. And of course, that I did not want to fall asleep at that moment, it was what I least wanted, having just experienced so much anguish and desperation. It was essential to reach the nearest village as soon as possible to seek for help. Notwithstanding, I now faced a fight of a completely different origin. I struggled to not close my eyes, but my eyelids were closing very slowly. I felt no pain whatsoever, just a great heaviness. It was as if a terrible tiredness was enwrapping me. After a couple more minutes, I could not avoid closing my eyes completely, and finally, I lost all knowledge of myself. I do not know for how long I was asleep, but when I opened my eyes again, I saw humanoid forms moving around me, and I got really scared. My vision was blurry, and I could not tell exactly what kinds of creatures were surrounding me. I could only see bulges and shadows moving around me. I knew they were living beings by the way they moved and communicated with each other, it was obvious. I could barely distinguish that they were making hand signs to each other, and I heard them making intelligent communication sounds. But I did not understand what they were saying. Instinctively, I wanted to get up to try to defend myself, but my body did not respond.

Thinking that the ape-men had finally reached us, panic ran through my mind, and I immediately tried to lift my sword. It was odd, but I did not feel my sword in my right hand anymore. Startled and extremely frightened, I tried to reach the dagger that was supposed to be attached to my left forearm (*the part of the arm between the wrist and elbow*). However, neither my hand nor my right arm responded to the order given by my brain. Furthermore, I could not feel that I had the dagger on my left forearm anymore. The idea that we had finally fallen prey to the harassment of the ferocious hunting group —*sank me in fear*.

Even so, I still had hope that I could defend myself because I remembered that I had one more spare weapon. Therefore, the next thing I did was trying to reach for the knife that I had fastened to my right thigh. Still, neither of my hands responded to the desire of my will. Likewise, I could not feel that I had that knife tied to my leg anymore. In a strange way, I also felt naked. Panic ran through me, for I felt completely helpless before the beings that surrounded me, and I had no idea why my body would not respond to my wishes and impulses. My eyesight just would not clear up. Suddenly, one of those beings carried me in its arms and handed me over to another creature. I could not do anything. I felt paralyzed and defeated. I was already expecting the worst…

KiD Vs SATAN

save your soul from hell!

My surprise was sudden when I heard a female voice that spoke to me in a sweet tone. The being hugged me with much delicateness and gently squeezed me against her chest, and as incredible as it may sound – *I could feel her love.* And I felt that her love was so great that even though I could not defend myself, and I did not know what was happening to me or where I was – *my intuition told me that this being would give even her own life for me if she had to, to protect me.* And that was the proof enough for me to know that I was in a safe place and among friends. Therefore, I closed my eyes and my **<<consciousness>>** rested. I was so tired that I gave myself back again to a profound sleep. It was a Tuesday in the month of September at eleven-fifteen in the morning, when I was born as a premature baby of seven months in the country and City of Mexico. The woman who held me in her arms was my own mother. This book is a Christian testimony, and in part, the autobiography of an atheist. For a long time, I wondered how I should start telling the story of my life. And after having spent several years thinking, I finally chose to start from the beginning – *with my very first memory of life on Earth.* Making this decision was not easy because I can only imagine what people are going to say. However, I will tell stories in this book that are even more fantastic than the previous story.

That is why I am fully aware that criticism will come at any time anyway.

Yet, as I said in the introduction, I will use the Bible as the basis for explaining my opinions and ideas, and the following verses will be the first ones I cite. These are located at:

Jeremiah 1:4-5. ***BEFORE I MADE YOU*** *in your mother's womb,* ***I KNEW YOU****.*
Before you were born, I chose you for a special work…

Romans 8:29. ***GOD KNEW THEM BEFORE HE MADE THE WORLD****. And he decided that they would be like his son. Then Jesus would be the firstborn of many brothers and sisters.*

Ephesians 1:4. ***BEFORE THE WORLD WAS CREATED****, God had Christ choose us to live with him and to be his holy and innocent and loving people.*

In these quotations:

—Do these scriptures tell us that God already knew us before we were born in this world?

—From where did God knows us already?

—Or, is it that we have lived in other times and still possibly in other lives?

—Or, rather, can we deduce that these scriptures tell us that God had us in his mind as futuristic beings who were going to be created one day on this world?

Any answer to these questions can become a hotly debated topic of discussion, where, in the end, there are people who would never agree on the meaning of all this. Consequently, I know that this issue will remain a **<<great>>** mystery. Therefore, my last memory of being pursued by beings that closely resembled the recreations I saw in illustrations of the Australopithecus afarensis (*in anthropology classes that I once took in college*) might have been just a dream.

And although the stories that are torn between what is true and false can deviate and get lost in uncertainty — I will continue this book telling the stories that actually have witnesses in this present life such as my family, brothers in Christ, and friends. And by making use of these real-life characters, I will better focus on the main theme of this writing. This is how a child in his ignorance came to challenge the Prince of Darkness, and how to save the soul from hell. Since I believe that this is a much more important objective to communicate at this moment.

To do this, I will describe many things that I have learned and seen over the course of my life, starting from my infancy. Let us begin…

PHYSICAL AND SPIRITUAL BODY

In the lessons that I have been taught in this life, I have learned that I have a physical body and a **<<spiritual>>** body. My physical or material body is easy to identify because it is my body of flesh and bone. The material body is a container. By that, I mean that my physical body is a receptacle or a storage unit for my spiritual body.

The spiritual body is difficult to identify because we cannot see it with the naked eye. I have already been out of my physical body, and for that reason, I know what my spiritual body looks like. The spiritual body is similar to the physical body in size and dimensions, therefore, it can be considered as a twin body. To that end, I am myself – *but in spirit* – and I live within my physical body.

In the exact same way, just as the body of flesh is the home of the spiritual body, the spiritual body is the dwelling for the **<<soul>>**. The soul is also difficult to identify because we cannot see it either. But the soul is easier to feel because the soul is the personality of the individual. Personality is the set of experiences, attitudes, thoughts, and feelings of a human being. The soul defines who you are as a person.

In short, a human being is composed of a physical body, a spiritual body, and a soul. But how did I reach such a conclusion? Well, the experiences in my own life have taught me so. Of course, that there are other clues that we can follow as well. For example, psychology has also struggled to explain that a human being consists of three parts. The way Doctor Sigmund Freud described it was by saying that a person has a mental state formed by *an id, an ego, and a super ego*. Simplifying, one can associate the *id* as the one who follows the desires of the flesh or, rather, the physical body. The *ego* can be the unconscious part or type of the spirit, and the *super-ego* would be the part that is the conscious and moral state of an individual or, rather, the soul.

Also, a doctor named Duncan MacDougall did experiments weighing people on a scale before and after their deaths. The results of his experiments indicated that a few minutes after dying, a person weighs about 0.74 ounces less than the person did before dying. The doctor concluded that at the death of an individual, the person's spirit leaves the physical body, and therefore the physical body weighs less. Following in the footsteps of the latter medics, there is a scientist in Russia, experimenting with technology to take pictures of the spirit leaving the physical body after death. This scientist has published a few books about his discoveries, and his name is Doctor Konstantin Korotkov.

Another doctor, named Raymond Moody, became well-known for writing a book containing the testimony of more than a hundred people who died clinically, and were then resurrected in a hospital. What the patients reported having seen after dying made of this good doctor one more believer in life after death. It is worth mentioning that the scientific discoveries of all these medical personalities named above are quite controversial. Still, of great interest. The Bible also talks about the difference and separation of – *the physical body and the spiritual body*. We can see an example here:

> *James 2:26. A person's **BODY** that **DOES NOT HAVE A SPIRIT** is **DEAD**...*

It seems clear what the scripture says. If the spiritual body is no longer inside the physical body, it is because the fleshly body has already died. I could go on quoting scriptures that show the separation and difference of the material body and the spiritual body. But if I quote too much from the holy scripture within this book, this text will become a miniature version of the Bible. And in order to make this content shorter, I will quote from one to a maximum of three quotations in each subject to help me explain my experiences, opinions, and ideas.

CHAPTER 2
CHILD
I SEE IT, YET, I DON'T BELIEVE IT

Some experiences I have had in my life have been somewhat emotionally traumatic, and I believe that is one of the reasons why I have been able to recall the incidents that I have lived, because they have been firmly imprinted in my memory. I have many memories from my early childhood, and I know that I have always considered myself a warrior. However, I will relate the experiences that are most relevant to the argument that I touch on this book. This is the explanation of how a child, in his ignorance, managed to challenge Satan, as well as the topic of the salvation of the soul. Some people think that when the physical body dies, life also ends. Although, in reality, this is not the case. Death can be the end of this life – *but it is not the conclusion of life itself as a whole*. When the physical body dies, the spiritual body leaves the fleshly body, meaning that life after death exists. I am a witness to that fact. Besides, I also bear witness to the fact that there exists a spiritual world, for I have seen it and I have even been there.

I began to experience the spiritual realm at a very young age.

Notwithstanding, I let the reader know that I had always refused to believe that the spiritual kingdoms called *Heaven* or *Hell* actually existed.

I refused to believe for fear of not being able to control things on which I had no power, and no knowledge whatsoever. For one or another reason, and despite the events I had seen with my own eyes, and even experienced in my own flesh, I did not want to believe that other realities existed.

I was among those who said:

—*If I do not see it, I will not believe it.*

The truth is that even though sometimes I was able to see some things that did not belong to this material world, I still did not believe in it. This could be one of the reasons why I became someone worse than a skeptic. I became a person who completely denied everything. Therefore, from saying:

—*If I do not see it, I will not believe it.*

With time, I came to say:

—*I see it… **But I do not believe it anyway**.*

From an early age, I developed a foolish and stubborn personality. And finally, over the years as I grew older, I became an atheist who tried to use scientific explanations, and educated reasoning to explain anything out of the ordinary.

Especially, I liked psychology a lot, and I took great interest and fondness into that branch of knowledge. Though, I have mentioned only some facts from my past to show the reader the type of personality I had before I meet the Lord Jesus, since I have not been always an admirer of and a faithful believer in him.

ONE UNUSUAL ENCOUNTER

I was three years old and I lived in a small house with my parents. The house was located in a community called San Cristobal, in the City of Mexico.

I remember that one day I was alone in my bedroom, and I found myself sitting on the floor and spending time with my toys.

It was just a regular day in the morning. The only window in the room was shut, but the window's curtains were open, and the sunlight flowed freely into my chamber. Therefore, the place where I was playing had enough light without needing an electric light bulb on for illumination.

I was very entertained playing with a small toy dinosaur when a **<<presence>>** manifested itself inside my bedroom. When I say *presence,* I mean someone, some being, or something that I could not explain because I could not see it, but only feel it.

At the exact moment that this presence appeared in my room, a small explosion echoed through the air. The things around me seemed to vibrate..., the bed, the mirror, the dresser, the closet, etc.

And even the particles in the air became clean, as if by an explosion or an electric discharge in the atmosphere.

It was as if that something or <<someone>> could not withstand impure particles, not even in the air, as tiny as these were, as it is the case of microbes or bacteria floating in the environment. And for this reason, apparently, even the very air was cleaned of any contamination.

I felt that someone was really there, and I think that this someone or something was watching me with great curiosity.

As I stared at a contact point into the <<nothingness>>, I felt that the *nothingness* was returning my look, and that it was cautiously staring back at me at the same time. But I could not see anybody. That presence was sustained in the ambiance, as if in the middle of my bedroom and above me. Of course, at least that was what I thought it was happening. I felt no fear. Still, I could sense that whatever that was flying in the middle of the air had – *real power* – and that I was completely defenseless before such might. That **<<enigmatic>>** presence began to visit me often in my room at this young age.

Regardless of it, this experience, far from making me feel afraid, made me feel protected because I started to believe, and to feel that someone was taking care of me.

PSYCHOLOGY OF CHILD 3-4

When I grew older, I liked to use psychology as a means of explaining the supernatural things that were happening to me. By finding a rational explanation for a paranormal event, I had always managed to avoid the anxiety of having to explain the facts or things that did not have a normal or a natural explanation. Each time I experienced something unusual, I would tell myself:

—I am not crazy. I think that I can explain what happened to me. This has to have a logical explanation.

And just as was I growing up, I was also inventing a thousand reasons and motives I could use to reject all of the supernatural experiences in my life. By doing that, I was able to manage and maintain my sanity, or at least a good enough state of mental health. In psychology, this self-defense action can be known as *self-preservation* and the act of maintaining good **<<self-esteem>>**. Self-preservation and the self-esteem principle are instincts built within each person (*are innate*). These instincts maintains, protects, and helps the human being to develop not only physically, but also at an emotional and at a mental level. That is to say, at a healthy psychological state. And, it is the job of the self-esteem to help every human to have a good concept of himself.

If an individual's self-esteem is low, that person tends to not transcend in life. For when a human being has a very low self-concept, that person tends to hold back, stagnate, and do not progress in life. Those who do not have a good self-esteem usually have all sorts of problems with themselves and with the people around them.

On the other hand, if an individual has a <<healthy>> self-esteem, the person manages to feel good about himself, and can develop better in life. That is why it is very important to preserve the self-esteem. In addition, psychology also argues that humans while growing up, pass through developmental periods that are not only physical (*corporal*), but also mental (*psychological*).

At each stage of development, human beings experience different psychological states as they grow and mature.

According to these stages of growth, a three-to-four years old infant experiences something very peculiar. Around this age is when children tend to create in their minds the so-called – *imaginary friend*. Some kids at this young age can be seen having long conversations with the aforementioned invisible friend.

As a young man, and while trying to explain my experiences as a child, I understood that this peculiarity among children of 3-4, could very well explain why I felt that presence visiting me.

Likewise, this same <<distinctiveness>> could also explain why I used to stare at fixed points where there was nobody, and why I felt that an invisible being – the imaginary friend – was looking after me. The more I learned about psychology, the more ways I learned to be happy with myself. For that reason, I always tried to explain the inexplicable – *to try to live happily and carefree.*

It is interesting to note that if a child has symptoms of being watched, the medical science does not take it too seriously. This is because it is well-documented that an infant can experience such things and it is taken as the brain is still developing at this early age. Moreover, if an adult presents the same symptoms, psychology could immediately classify such behavior as a **<<paranoia>>**.

Paranoia is a personality disorder in which the individual can imagine things, like being watched or feeling persecuted, and therefore, the person could feel endangered.

In a separate opinion, some psychologists might say that the hallucinations that some kids have are just another way they can express themselves. This could help them to test the boundaries of the new world that they are about to experience. Children, perhaps consciously or subconsciously, may seek which are the earthly laws that will help them to live, and to meet the challenges of this life.

In this way, the child may find himself through fantasies, and he does that in a harmless way through playing. The parents, in turn, are the ones who must guide the little one by marking the boundaries between fantasy and reality. And they need to do this, without, at the same time, cutting the wings of the kid's imagination. The child must experience a healthy childhood in order to achieve a maximum potential while maturing to his adult stage. An overly exaggerated criticism by the parents could end up damaging this delicate level of development. Another thing I remember from that early age is that sometimes I started to cry suddenly, and without any apparent motive. I remember clearly that when I was three-to-four years old, I asked myself:

—*Why do I cry?*

—*Does something hurt in my body?*

And I answered my own question as well:

—*No, nothing really hurts.*

Then I continued on checking the physical status of my body, and similarly I responded:

—*I am neither hungry, nor thirsty.*

—*Yet I am crying! What is happening to me?*

After that, I answered:

—*Well, it must be a state of development of this brain and body.*

And I think that I was not too far from the truth because psychology has an explanation for that situation as well. Let us see…

The science of the mind tells us that a child at this age can suffer from abrupt changes of mood. The minor can be happy at one moment and be crying the next instant, and what happens is that this is a stage of a child's emotional development. I remember experiencing this kind of behavior, and also of my thoughts when I was that young. That is why, it occurs to me to offer the following advice to every parent:

—*Parents please do not beat your children if they happen to cry a lot.*

—*Remember that this could very well be a state of brain development, and of the development of the emotional state of the infant.*

THE POSSESSION

The next out-of-the-ordinary experience that I remember happened when I was four years old. My mother's name is *Mary of Socorro*. I remember that one evening somewhere around seven o'clock, I thought I saw and heard my mother crying in her room. That late in the evening the room was already somewhat dark, its lights were turned off, and its only windows were already closed for the cold of the night was starting to make its presence felt. However, there was a bit of light coming from a light bulb from the courtyard of the house, so some scarce light infiltrated through the pale yellow, and very transparent window's curtains.

In the dim light, I could see the dark figure of my mother sitting at the edge of the bed. The silhouette was bent forward, facing the window with her back towards me, and the palms of her two hands were over her face like if she was sobbing. And even though she was crying softly, I could very well hear her lament.

Finding this situation unusual, I wanted to approach my mother to see what was wrong. Full of curiosity, I entered her room slowly and quietly…

When I approached my mother to see why she was crying – *something jumped* – from the bulge that appeared to be my mother, and I felt that whatever it was had hit me right on the chest. It felt as if a strong blast of air had entered the upper part of my body. I got scared, therefore I immediately ran out of the room. But at the same time, and from then on, I began to feel <<hatred>> in my heart. I am aware that I was a spoiled and a very hot-tempered child. Nevertheless, since that incident, I know that I started to hate humankind.

I think that my whole life changed a lot, as did my personality on that day because I became a bad kid. Or rather, I should say, not just bad but *malevolent*. It is my own personal belief and opinion that at that precise moment of my childhood, I was **<<possessed>>** by an unclean spirit.

Yes, by a demon.

Granting that I was only a four-year-old child, it is clear that I had no knowledge of spiritual possessions, nor of demons. Hence, I preferred to forget the incident. In any case, at this age, I would not have known how to explain myself. No one would have understood or believed me, and no one could have helped me. My family was not religious, and we scarcely ever attended church back then.

PSYCHOLOGY OF CHILD 4-5

According to the psychology applied to the stages of growth of a person, a four-to-five years old child still does not recognize the danger of crossing a street without paying attention to the cars. Neither does he pay attention to many other dangers. Consequently, the little one is very impulsive in his actions, because he still cannot measure the risks.

Infants at this age also tend to be very selfish because it is hard for them to process the concept of sharing. It is assumed that children of four to five years old can already express themselves with words, and therefore they can avoid physical aggression with their little friends. Also, kids at this young age tend to find the so-called best friend from among their schoolmates or playmates.

Nevertheless, the above description did not entirely explain me. For I was very aggressive at that age, and it was fun for me to fight with other kids. And that about making friends was not my situation either, because let's just say that children did not like to approach me very much... For obvious reasons.

CHAPTER 3

MY BROTHER MUST DIE!

While many five-years-old children think only about playing, at that age I was already contemplating the idea of how to kill my younger brother. My younger brother's name is *Gabriel*. I was five years old and my little brother was only three years old at that time. I wanted to kill my brother because I could not bear the idea of sharing the love and affection of my parents with him. The **<<hatred>>** blinded me, so I decided to kill my brother, and I waited for the right moment to come by.

It happened that one day when my mother was asleep and my little brother was inside his crib. I thought that this was the perfect moment because the snotty little brat could not escape me. I went to the kitchen drawer and I took an icepick (*pointed and sharp metal instrument*). After that, I entered my brother's room, and closed the door quietly. Then I went up into his crib, and I took my brother by the neck with my left hand, and with my right hand holding the ice pick, I stabbed him as many times as I could.

The infant started to cry and to shout while I contemplated how his clothes began to soak with his own blood. However, I did not stop. I just wanted my brother dead and to get him out of my house. Thank God that my mother heard the cries of my helpless brother, and came opportunely to save little *Gabriel*. Notwithstanding, that was only the beginning of many years of fighting between my brother and me because we became harsh, bitter enemies. When my brother grew up and could defend himself from me, we became the full personification of the dog against the cat. We used to fight by hitting, kicking, biting, punching, and cursing at each other – every single day. Sadly, my parents were never able to make us behave like brothers and as educated people. The thing my parents did in their desperation to try control me was to beat me, and that only fueled the hatred that was already living in my heart.

At five years old, I became a disobedient, rebellious, and very aggressive child. I caused an untold number of problems for my parents because I liked to fight against other children and making mischief. I remember that each night, and already in my bed, I **<<enjoyed>>** myself thinking about the wicked things that I would do when the sun rose.

I thought that maybe breaking a window, burning a toy, or maybe beating up some kid would be fun. I also developed a special taste for the thing called – *revenge*.

Back then, I believed myself to be stronger than the other children were, and I also felt a great sense of delight in my heart by misbehaving. In particular, I felt great joy inside myself when I made someone cry and suffer. For me, hatred was **<<pleasure>>** and causing suffering to someone was something good to do, and I tried every day to feed that *enjoyment* in my heart.

And so, I lived my life from an early childhood surrounded by the problems of bad behavior and bad attitude. I caused all types of frustrations for my parents, and for people who had the bad luck of being my next victims because my evil deeds were many.

My father's name is *Joseph Louis*, and one of those days I heard my mother telling my father:

– Joseph Louis, when this child grows up, he is going to kill people.

I know that my mother was very preoccupied with me and the direction that my life would take in the future. For I was very difficult to control, and she had no training or knowledge, nor any power to help me. Now let us read the following passage:

> *Isaiah 5:20-21.* You are headed for trouble! **YOU SAY WRONG IS RIGHT, DARKNESS IS LIGHT**, and bitter is sweet. You think you are clever and smart.

What was written in the previous scripture was precisely my situation. That was my real life in those days.

Those people, who walk in the path of wickedness, do exactly the opposite of God's will, but still they dare to call it <<good>>.

How can I best explain my behavior at that age? At the age of five, and according to my own way of thinking, I was doing what was right because I was doing what felt good inside me. As long as I could satisfy my inner needs, nothing else seemed to have something of importance.

I know that it is hard to believe, but there are adults who have the same type of personality that I had when I was that age. Unfortunately, there are people who stay trapped in that stage of development.

This type of people does not experience progress in their personalities, and they remain stuck there. Because by continuing in that state, they feel safe and confident in themselves, and they also perceive that they have a – certain control – over their lives, and over the people who surround them.

In some way, they consider that they have achieved **<<success>>** in life by behaving like that, and satisfied with that, this is how they have chosen to stay, live and die.

These types of people exist. I was one of them. At that time, I was greatly mistaken in my appreciation of life.

My father *Joseph Louis* is an electrical engineer. One day he was hired to work on the electrical maintenance of a factory that extracted metal from a mountain. This iron mine is still located to this day in a town called The Pearl, in the state of Chihuahua, Mexico. The township of The Pearl, is just a small settlement located in plain desert. It is surrounded by bold and arid hills because it hardly ever rains and the vegetation is scarce there. When we moved into this town, I joined the kindergarten (*preschool*), since I was still around five years old. Already taking classes in the kindergarten, I felt I was superior to my classmates. I thought I was stronger, faster, and smarter than they were. In my imagination, I was the supreme leader and the commander in chief of the school, and the child who would dare to disobey me, I would beat him up – easy fix. Now I had officially become a schoolyard bully.

PSYCHOLOGY OF CHILD 5-6

Per the developmental stages of a child's growth, a five-to-six years old kid usually tends to show care and affection to people younger than he is or towards children who suffer from some pain. The little one at this age is generally obedient to his parents or caregivers. Well, none of that was my case because I behaved exactly the opposite of that description at that age.

VOICES WITHOUT A BODY

At the age of six, I had another strange experience again. I enjoyed to sing, and back then there was a Spanish folk song that I liked a lot. That melody is called *Veronica.* The name of the artist who interpreted it on the radio was *Victor Iturbe the Piruli.*

At that time, I thought that this was the best song in the entire world, and that no other melody created before or after would be just as good. That ballad made me feel closer to **<<love>>** than anything else. That is why I used to sing that song while walking down the streets. One day, I said to myself:

—*I wish I had nice feelings so I could compose beautiful songs like Veronica.*

And while walking and thinking about such things — a voice — came to my left ear and offended me with the next words:

—*Damn you!*

After coursing, the voice questioned me:

—*What did you just say?*

—*An evil man like you? A human with so much hatred, a being so perverse, and such a wrongdoer... How is it that you are requesting something so noble, and that requires such good feelings?*

After that, the voice, in a provocative tone, ultimately mentioned:

– *It is stupid of you to ask for such a thing!*

After telling me this, the voice replied with a resounding and mocking burst of laughter. The guffaw was completely malevolent and mercilessly made fun of my good wishes. At that moment, I felt ridiculed and very small inside. Because that voice was right. It was like asking for beautiful and delicate colorful flowers to a plant that could only give poisonous acid. Only a **<<miracle>>** could put nice feelings inside me. My simple dreams of having enough good feelings as to write a love song, seemed not just completely absurd, but unreachable as well. Therefore, and after all, I was not surprised. That voice in my left ear was not telling me anything anew. I was well aware of the miserable state of my humanity at that moment in life.

However, what did surprise me was that it seemed as if – someone else – was apparently listening or reading my thoughts at that instant. What is more, that *someone* was well aware of the allegations of the voice talking in my ear and making fun of me.

And while the mocking laughter persevered against me relentlessly, it happened that another voice became present. Nonetheless, this voice was different.

This voice was hovering over my head and headed for my right ear.

And, as if the message was not only for me but also for someone else, with an energetic statement, the new voice said shouting:

—I will make your petition to having nice feelings for writing songs be heard!

And as the scandalous voice was saying that, it faded rapidly, heading towards the sky and to the white clouds that looked like a soft and shiny cotton under the sunlight. I turned my face upward and then sideways, though, I never saw anyone.

At that point, I wondered whether my head was okay, or if, in addition to all the problems that I already had, now I was starting to go crazy.

I am aware that the condition of — hearing voices — can be categorized in psychology as a **<<schizophrenia>>**. A *schizophrenic* person hears and sees hallucinations. For the schizophrenic, it is hard to distinguish what is truth from what is a hallucination. But once again, is interesting to note that if such a peculiarity occurs in some children sporadically, the medical science does not take it too seriously. After all, there are a few children who have those experiences with some regularity. Such is the recurrence, that these experiences can be considered as part of their infancy, part of their growth, and part of their evolving imagination.

For the reason that the child's brain continues its biological development.

PSYCHOLOGY OF CHILD 6-7

Per the stages of growth and maturation of a person, a little one of six-to-seven years old still has problems with being aware of the concept of morality or ethical behavior. A minor of six years old tends to be very curious and likes to ask about all the things around him. At this stage, the kid increasingly suffers from a fear of the dark and of strange noises because the child already believes in magic and in fantasy. Therefore, children can already imagine monsters in the dark.

Applying the above description to my experiences of when I was that age, I became aware that it was fairly easy to blame the child's imagination for making me hallucinate of those voices.

Disembodied voices that talked to me? Voices accusing me of wrongdoings? Voices that faded while rising into the sky? No, of course not, it was pure fantasy… I reasoned.

CHAPTER 4
THE INVISIBLE MASTER

After a short while, I was already seven years old, but my life was still the same. Correction, rather, I should have said that my life had taken a turn for the worse. I was a problem child wherever I was. At seven years old, I thought that my pranks, and mischiefs had already surpassed the limit of endurance some time long ago. And I asked myself:

—*How is it that my parents can suffer me so much?*

Then I continued saying:

—*If I had a son like me, I would have strangled him already!*

I also remember that at that age, I only kept complaining about my daily life and about my miserable **<<existence>>**. I complained because I could not conduct myself in a proper way, and I even enjoyed misbehaving, and as you can imagine dear reader, that caused me a lot of problems. Unusual was the day when I was not punished or beaten up at home because I had done something wrong. Thus, I wondered why my life had to be like that.

Why did I behave like an animal or worse than an animal that does not understand?

I used to fistfight with one or another child almost every day. The day that I would not scuffle into a brawl with someone, I felt like my body needed to be beaten anyway. For that reason, I grabbed a leather belt and I lashed myself on my back with the metal of the belt's buckle. To inform the reader, the act of self-punishment with any instrument is called **<<flagellation>>**. Hence, I practiced *flagellation* when I was alone in my room. I was not afraid of being battered, rather, I needed it to sleep satisfied with my day to day life. Every day I kept asking myself if my entire life would be like that, and I was anxious to know:

—Why can I not understand reasons, and obey my parents and teachers at school?

Then, I began to realize and believe that my existence on Earth would be only unhappy and pathetic.

In the same way, I came to understand that there was nothing for me in this life – neither at that moment nor in the future. At night before going to sleep, I watched television, and seeing the news depressed me even more. Since I noticed that there were too many problems in this planet, and that made me wonder why so much evil existed. I could perceive that I lived in an imperfect and extremely cruel world.

Because of this, I daily asked myself the next questions…

—Why is there so much pain, death, poverty, and robbery?

—Why does so much disease exist, and war everywhere?

—From where do all the catastrophes and all the corruption come from?

Oh, and I do not want to forget that I also wondered:

—Why are there so many awful smells in this world?

And there were no answers, but only anxiety and plenty of frustration.

There have been several moments and stages in my life when I have had personal philosophies that I have repeated daily, something like a mantra or mania. My personal saying at that moment in life was:

—I do not want to live here, and I do not want to live this life!

I used to say that daily. I was spending each moment denying my own existence, for I was disillusioned about everything I saw. The bad news on television, my own bad behavior, and my sick attitude towards life made me see only a world that was brutal and hostile to any benevolence.

I had no respect for life. I felt an exquisite pleasure in causing pain to people and in killing all sorts of animals in the hills of the town. I had no regrets. There was no light at the end of the tunnel. There was no hope for me.

And if this planet was full of people just like me, then, there was no hope for this world either. Sadly, that was my way of thinking at the young age of seven years old. Ever since childhood, I have always enjoyed being alone. For some reason, I had great affection for solitude. One of those days I went out alone, hunting and killing animals on the mountains that surrounded the town. Lonely, I wandered through the hills, going my way, complaining about all the bad things I found in this life – as it was already my habit. So, I walked around like this, muttering, complaining, and cursing. I did not keep it to myself. I was loud about it. Simply, I did not want to live anymore, and the entire world had to know it. It was a cloudy day. It had just rained, which was unusual for the desert. The scent of wet soil could be smelled in the air. The sun hesitated to come out, and hid its radiant glow behind one after another wandering gray cloud. By then, it was about two o'clock in the afternoon when suddenly, and without any warning – *an invisible being* – started talking to me. I saw no one standing near me, but a voice started talking into my ears in a clear, friendly, and warm tone.

The invisible being was talking to me as if he had known me from a long time ago, and his voice inspired trust and friendship. The voice seemed to be from a young man, and apparently, judging by the sound coming from the voice, the man was taller than I was.

I turned my head around searching for the whereabouts of the voice, but there was no one standing next to me. Despite that, I had no fear. Not because I was very brave but because I think that my experience of hearing voices *without seeing a body* when I was six years old, had already made me somewhat familiar with this kind of occurrence.

However, the invisible being apparently **<<knew>>** my thoughts. What is more, he knew not only my thoughts of that instant, but apparently also my thoughts from a very long time ago. In brief, when that voice started talking to me, it said:

—*Why do you lament so much? The only thing I hear from you day and night is complaints and you do not stop whining!*

After that, the invisible being continued saying:

—*Just as you say there is hatred, there is also love. Just as well as there are bad smells, what do you say about the aroma of the roses? What do you say about the fragrance of exquisite perfumes? Just as there are bad people, there are also good people. Just as there are thieves and dishonesty...*

Here the voice took on a more energetic tone, but continued saying with joy:

—*There are also people who seek truth and justice! Just as there is death... There is life! Just as there is pain and sorrow... There is also happiness! What do you say about the joy of laughter?*

Afterwards, raising his voice a little more which by then it already carried a reproach tone, the invisible apparition added:

—*You see only the bad because you are being obstinate. Do not you know that you have to live this life anyway?*

—*Then, what good is it for you to complain so much? But I will tell you more...* (the exceptional teacher proceeded).

—*If you insist on living this life, thinking about negative things, you will be able to live life* (here the voice paused and later continued) ..., *but you will not be happy.*

—*I will let you know that you can also pledge to live this life thinking about positive things. You can live life that way as well. The difference is that you will be happy instead.*

—*The* **<<secret>>** *to happiness is to take the road to happiness. There is only one way to it, and only you have the choice to choose this path and no one else.*

—*Remember this very well... You are already in this world, you have to live this life, and only you make the decision to be happy or unhappy.*

The invisible being finally exclaimed:

— *Everything is in you!*

And the lesson stopped right there. Just as suddenly as the voice had come, it disappeared, and I stood alone, not knowing what to make of it all. It may be surprising to someone, but the Bible tells us about the experience of hearing voices in the ear. We can see that in the next page.

> *Job 33:16-18.* ***HE*** *may* ***WHISPER*** *something* ***IN THEIR EAR****, and they are frightened when they hear his warnings.* ***GOD WARNS*** *people to stop them from doing wrong and to keep them from becoming proud. He does this* ***TO SAVE THEM*** *from death.*

I have always read books since childhood, for I have persistently sought the answers to life, just as many people question themselves. Yet, when I read what the Bible says in the verse listed above, I felt – goose bumps – on the back of my head. According to the scriptures, God himself can talk in someone's hear! The lessons that the Bible can give us are striking. Still, many times we read the scripture and we do not understand it because we lack the spiritual **<<discernment>>**. Sometimes spiritual *discernment* is acquired when God makes you live an experience in your own life, and then later, after reading the Bible, you can say…

–Oh… I get it!

Then, one thing it is to read the Bible and another one to understand it. It is also one thing to understand the Bible and quite another to experience it or to live it. It is sad, but most people do not understand the sacred scriptures, and therefore, do not live the word of God found in it.

With this book I hope to put my two cents in on the subject, and perhaps help someone to understand some quotations. I have confidence that the biblical citations that you will learn in this text, will give you the knowledge necessary and sufficient to save your soul from hell, and have a personal encounter with God.

PSYCHOLOGY OF CHILD 7-8

A normal child of this age shows more sympathy and kindness with respect to the problems and needs of those around him. The little on also tends to be less selfish and show more cooperation with his family. In addition, the kid can become more reserved or introverted. The idea of failing and not succeeding in life already lurks in the mind of the minor by that time.

In my situation, I was not kind at all, and I behaved in a very selfish way. All of this was combined with a lack of willingness on my part to cooperate with my family because – *I hated everyone* –. Still and all, I knew that something bad was happening to me. Something was very wrong with me, but I did not know what it was, and I was really worried about my future.

DICHOTOMY OF LIFE

Life on Earth has a dichotomy. Dichotomy means having to make a choice between two opposing decisions. There is a dichotomy when we choose between having positive thoughts or negative thoughts. In a like manner, we could say that there is a dichotomy when we choose between doing good and doing bad. In reality, we do this so frequently that we no longer pay much attention to it. In this moment, the important thing is to know that this mental action exists and that it occurs in our brains a great number of times during the day. After the lesson that the singular invisible master gave me, I decided to give it a try being a positive person. Dear reader, I am quite slow to learn, but I was quick to put that lesson into practice, and when I stopped complaining so much, my life changed in a certain way. I noticed that I began to live a little happier without so much turmoil within my thoughts.

In the next pages, I will discuss the **<<four>>** steps that were shown to me to live better, and that are also of great help in seeking, knowing God, and obtaining salvation of the soul. The first step is…

KID
VS
SATAN
HOW TO SAVE YOUR SOUL FROM HELL
(REAL LIFE STORY)

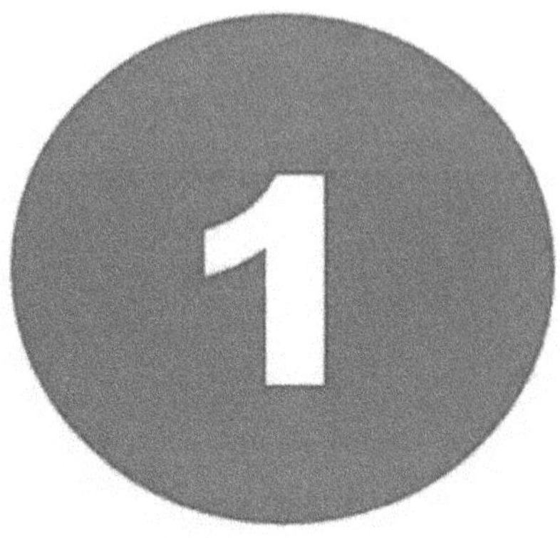

FIRST STEP TO SAVE THE SOUL

The first step is – **Be Positive**. Think and speak only about good things. Remember that thinking and speaking good things are actions that must go – hand in hand – to make this work. Talking and thinking good things, are not, nor will they be two separate things for this to be in agreement with God. Let us see what the Bible says with respect to this issue:

> *Deuteronomy 5:28-29. The Lord heard what you said and told me, 'I heard what the people* ***SAID****. And that is* ***FINE****. I only wanted to change their way of* ***THINKING****-I wanted them to respect me and obey all my commands from the heart. Then everything would be fine with them and with their descendants forever.*

Here in the book of Deuteronomy, Moses describes an act by the Jewish people. The scripture tells us that God seemed pleased by what the people said. Therefore, it means that the people – were speaking good things. Afterwards, God said that he would like for the people to always *think* well. The result of speaking well and thinking well, as the citation puts it, is that the people will be better. The scripture says that the persons will have a fine life or a happy life. The things you think and talk about are so **<important>** to God that the same lesson repeats itself in many chapters throughout the Bible:

> *Matthew 12:35-37. Those who are good have good things saved in their hearts. That's why they* **SAY GOOD THINGS**. *But those who are evil have hearts full of evil, and that's why they say things that are evil. I tell you that everyone will have to answer for all the careless things they have said. This will happen on the day of judgment.* **YOUR WORDS WILL BE USED TO JUDGE YOU**. *What you have said will show whether you are right or whether you are guilty."*

> *Genesis 6:5. The Lord saw that the people on the earth were very evil. He saw that* **THEY THOUGHT** *only about* **EVIL THINGS ALL** *the* **TIME**.

These scriptures teach us that God **<<actually>>** hears everything we say and think. For this reason, it is extremely important that we pay attention to it. Hence, it is better to wish only good things with your mind, and to also speak only good things.

It may surprise you to learn that according to a recent study from the National Science Foundation (*NSF*), a person with a busy mind can have anywhere from twelve thousand to fifty thousand thoughts per day. Similarly, it is interesting to note that the same study reveals that up to eighty percent of those thoughts are usually negative.

If this is so, then there is some true to the biblical recommendation. Human beings can be quite negative in their thoughts. Therefore, people will have to change their way of thinking if they want to see the spiritual kingdom called Heaven. Once you convert those negative thoughts into positive thoughts, and the bad words into good words, you will be closer to the salvation of your soul, and you will be walking firmly to the second step.

CHAPTER 5

ME AS A PRIEST?

Now I was eight years old and apparently, the encounter with the invisible being and the teaching of behaving as a positive person had left me pretty enthusiastic. That is why, I began to visit the church with frequency. There was only one temple in the town. The parish was Catholic, and it was very small, but I gladly attended it every Sunday morning. I remember well that at that age, I used to ask myself about which profession I would pursue in the future. What would be the best-paid job? Perhaps it would be a good idea to become a lawyer. Or what about becoming a famous actor?

I also dreamed of working as an ambassador for my country in some exotic and distant foreign land. I pictured myself carrying an expensive portfolio made of crocodile skin. I would wear an expensive suit and fine silk ties. My suit, a light gray color, would be made of the coveted cashmere wool, and tailored by a famous designer.

My shoes would be wine colored and made of a high-shine patent leather.

My work's office would have to look like the one of a great successful executive. For I would have a luxurious desk made of expensive wood of mahogany, and palm trees all around inside the office, because I really like vegetation and plants.

On the other hand, I also remember thinking about the likelihood of the reality of God, and I used to say to myself:

—*If God does exist, he would be the greatest boss on the entire planet.*

—*In that case, would it not be better paid and more important to work for the greatest boss there is?*

Despite of my profound thoughts about the possible existence of the divinity or about my plans to get established as an important public servant, I was still behaving as badly as I possibly could. By that time, the town of The Pearl had gone a full month without television. This was because I had set fire to the only one antenna that received and transmitted the television signal in the small town. The day was too short to do wickedness and that included playing one or another little cruel prank.

SOME BAD NEWS

I had an uncle named *Anthony*, who lived with his family in the Mexican state of Michoacan in a city called Lazaro Cardenas. One day we received the terrible news that my uncle *Anthony* had prematurely passed away at just thirty-five years of age. His death had been a bit unusual because he died while undergoing a simple surgical removal of the tonsils (*tonsillectomy*). After the doctor had administered anesthesia to begin the surgery, *Anthony* fell asleep, and did not wake up again.

This event was particularly painful for many people because my uncle was an excellent provider for his family, a good husband, and a noble father. I remember my uncle as an extremely kind and a very nice person.

My uncle was survived by his wife, my aunt *Hortensia,* his two daughters, my cousins *Elizabeth and Theresa,* and his son, my cousin *Tony*. My aunt *Hortensia* was the sister of my father *Joseph Louis*. That is the reason why, the children of my aunt *Hortensia* are my full cousins. My cousins and I are roughly the same age, so we always played together when our parents visited each other.

PSYCHOLOGY OF CHILD 8-9

According to the growth and maturity stages of psychology, a little one at this age usually enjoys socializing with other people, and especially likes to spend time with his own family. Despite this, a child of eight to nine years old can be impatient and obnoxious at times. The minor may like to criticize and argue with his parents and may also be somewhat rude. The reason for this could be that the kid may feel inadequate and maybe even unhappy with his economic status, because at this age children already begin making comparisons of social class.

Something special that happens at this stage, is that a child has trouble accepting guilt or accepting that he has done something wrong. At the age of eight-to-nine years, when the minor makes a mistake, he usually defends himself by blaming someone or something else. The choices between good and evil occupy much of the little boy's mind at this period.

In my case, I experienced the normal things that a lad experiences at this age, with the exception being that I had zero skills at socializing with people.

THE OTHER DIMENSIONS

At this point in time in the story, I was already nine years old, and my family and I had moved to live to the City of Mexico. We lived in an apartment complex. To this day this building is still located in the municipality called Obrera, on a street named Elizabeth the Catholic, and just a few minutes away from the principal governmental square called the Zocalo.

My life remained pretty much the same. I kept fighting with my classmates and with children around the neighborhood, and when I was back home, I was giving my parents and my brother *Gabriel* a hard time. This was because I was still full of hatred and of rebellion. By then my aunt *Hortensia* and her children had also moved to the City of Mexico, and they lived relatively close to my apartment. One day my parents visited my aunt *Hortensia's* house, and it happened that my cousins *Elizabeth* and *Theresa* invited me to play a special game with them. It was a fun pastime that they had been using for entertainment for a while – the famous game of the Ouija board. And perhaps the reader may ask, What is a Ouija board?

The Ouija board is a game that consists of a flat and square wooden table with the following things written on it – the letters of the alphabet, the numbers from 0-9, and the words Yes, No, and Goodbye. It is said that only the true psychic mediums can use the Ouija board to communicate with the dead. I played with the game of the Ouija board only while visiting my cousins considering that I really did not believe in it. However, my cousin *Theresa* had taken a keen **<<interest>>** in it, and played the game quite often. She began to consult with the Ouija board when she was only eight years old, because she believed that through this game it was possible to talk to her father, who had passed away some time before.

At first, the spirit inside the Ouija board assured my cousin that he was her late father. For that reason, *Theresa* played to communicate with the spirit of her father for several hours daily.

Summoning a spirit in a game session on the Ouija board was extremely easy for both of my cousins. By lightly placing a couple of fingers on a small wooden heart, asking a question to the board, and by concentrating intently, one could make a *spirit* respond by moving the wooden heart over the tablet. The wooden heart stopped pointing at each letter, forming words that in turn formed complete sentences. To give dates and hours, the wooden heart stopped on the numbers from 0 to 9.

The Ouija board, which seemed to be only an – innocent game – to have for fun for a while, turned out to be a whole nightmare for the small family of my aunt *Hortensia*.

In the beginning, *Theresa* lived her life as she normal did, but the day came when my cousin began to behave in a very unusual way. The sweet dream that she had restored the communication with her late beloved father became a horrific **<<nightmare>>**. That was because a demon began appearing in her dreams while she slept, and the satanic creature intimidated her by saying:

–I have come for you, you belong to me, you are mine.

The beast that appeared to her had the face of a goat, with a long black beard. From his skull protruded a pair of twisted horns that, like molten sulfur, were reddish yellow in color. The horns showed patches of black ash stains in some parts of the turns. His eyes were incandescent red, like burning coals.

From his snout emerged a pair of long, curved, and pointed canine fangs of a dirty ivory color. With the exception of his head, the upper part of his body (*the torso*) was like that of a man, while the lower part of his body was like that of a goat. The entity had hairy dark brown legs that ended with scorched and opaque black hooves. His fur glistened. From all of his body emanated a heavy and foul-smelling gray smoke.

As the time passed by, the unclean spirit not only intimidated her with words, but also began to attack her and to hurt her during her dreams. During the night, when *Theresa* was screaming in terror and pain over what she was experiencing in her nightmares, her over-excited mother would run into her daughter's room, trying to help. Anyhow, all efforts were in vain. The nightmares kept repeating themselves at night, and nobody could do anything to help my cousin.

For a while, the nightmares tormented her only while she was sleeping at night. But later, the suffering was not only during the night, but also during the day. My cousin began to faint during daytime. When she fainted and later regained consciousness, her mouth emitted the sounds of animals, and her gaze changed. Her face wrinkled and her eyes looked angry. Furthermore, she could not recognize the people around her. She was not even able to identify her own family, and *Theresa* would say to us:

—*Who are you?*

—*Where I am?*

And something shocking is that her strength was so great. Not even five men were strong enough to take her to Sunday's service, because she resisted and was stronger than they were. Little by little, among family and friends, my cousin started to gain a reputation of being **<<crazy>>**.

However, when her mother took *Theresa* to consult with many specialists, as strange as it may seem, neither the physicians nor the psychiatrists could find any disease in her.

If psychology tries to explain the kind of nightmares of being chased, being bitten by an animal, or being killed – it is said that the common cause may be that the person has problems with social adaptation. In the same way, and also according to psychology, a nightmare may be a normal reaction to the amount, and type of stress to which an individual is subject in his daily live.

If the problem continues and prevents the social development of the person, then the situation can be considered as a **<<disorder>>** or a disturbance. And if the nightmare is recurring with the same subject, then the problem could have been classified as a type of disorder named *repetitive nightmare*. It is worth noting that this type of problem is more common in women than in men. Therefore, according to the science of the mind, all this could have a scientific explanation. Or could it?

In my opinion, the Ouija board is not a <<game>> as innocently is portrayed by the toy stores. In reality, the Ouija board is a door – *it is a spiritual portal to a malignant dimension* – since all sorts of evil spirits can come out of that object.

Let us look at what the Bible has to say on this subject on the next page…

> *Leviticus 19:31.* ***DO NOT*** *go to mediums or wizards for advice –* ***THEY WILL*** *only* ***MAKE YOU UNCLEAN****. I am the Lord your God.*

As one can read in the scripture, starting from thousands of years ago, God has been giving advice to people to help them to avoid problems. God knows all too well that by invoking spirits, a person will become **<<unclean>>**. In other words, that the spirit of the person who invokes the spirit of the dead *will contaminate* itself with the spirit that has been summoned. What this really means is that a person can accommodate another spirit in his fleshly body, defiling himself that way.

And this type of damage cannot be detected by the person simply by looking with the naked eye, because it happens in a spiritual plane. If a person, after playing the Ouija board, could see a **<<monkey>>** hanging from his neck, then, who in their right mind would play with it? Well, it is clear that this is not that obvious.

In *Theresa's* special situation, what happened is that a demon was impersonating as her late father *Anthony*.

Over time, and after building trust and friendship with my cousin, the evil spirit finally left the Ouija board – to then take possession inside of Theresa's physical body.

And if the reader asks, how is it that there is a place for a spirit within the body of a person? Well, what happens is that the physical body is a – container or a receptacle – for the spiritual body.

Occasionally, a person can feel an empty space in his or her chest, this is the place I am referring to. The body of flesh can accommodate other spirits besides the human spirit itself. And, as incredible as it may seem, the human body can accommodate thousands of demonic spirits within. This can happen because a spiritual body is not subject to the physical laws of a material body. As an example of what I say, we have what has been biblically written in the book of Mark chapter five – when Christ cast away the demonic yoke from the possessed man of Gerasenes. Let us look at what the next scripture says:

> *Mark 5:9. Then Jesus asked the man, "What is your name?"*

If you can read the whole chapter in the Bible, you will see that it **<<seems>>** as if Jesus asked this question of the man. But, in reality the question was meant for the evil spirit within the man. How big was the surprise when the answer of the demon was…

—My name is legion because there are many spirits inside.

What is more, it is interesting to note that a Roman legion in the time of Jesus was composed of as many as six thousand soldiers. To make matters worse, not only a human being can be infested with evil spirits — just as cockroaches can invade a house — but also, from my own experience I let you know, that a person with a demonic possession may experience problems that can <<escalate>>. What I mean by this, is that the person's problems can gradually increase, and to such an extent that over time the individual can even lose the will to live. This can happen because the demon has the power to take away the taste for living from the person.

Likewise, it is also important to make known that it is always a futile effort to try to make friends with an unclean entity. As these are deceptive creatures that have only the intention of destroying humans or the complete **<<annihilation>>** of the being of which they take possession of.

As an example of what I say, you can look again in Mark chapter five, with verse thirteen. What you can see in that scripture, is that when the legion of evil spirits came out of the possessed man, they went immediately into a herd of pigs. What followed was that the legion of demons made the herd to commit suicide, as the hogs ran into a lake and drowned.

Although, most of the time, the unclean spirit kills the person of whom it has taken possession of, in a more delicate or much more subtle way— so to speak. In view of the fact that, in a human being, the demon acts slowly suffocating its victim. Like this, little by little, the infernal being takes away the victim's pleasure in living and can constantly harass the person with suicidal thoughts. Nevertheless, you should never question whether if the demons would like to kill a human being as quickly as they killed the pigs, as in the last example from the Bible. This is because Satan and his fallen angels hate and detest with all of their guts the naive and skeptical homo sapiens (*wise human*).

One of the differences between a human being and an animal is that a human has autonomy in other words —free will — while animals do not. The malignant spirit can put the desire for suicide into the human mind, but overcoming the human willingness is harder for the demon. Unfortunately, animals do not have such defense considering that they act only on instinct. Ultimately, demons are not friends of anyone, and if they do show friendship, it is only to pretend. They do this in order to take down the person's defenses so that they can approach the individual. These detestable beings only wish the destruction of humanity in its entirety.

The name of their diabolical game is: **<<Control and Destruction>>**.

Concerning the use of objects to make a spiritual contact, this is not a good idea either and I will explain why I say so. With the words – objects of contact – I refer to anything a person can use as an accessory to communicate with another dimension. A contact artifact becomes a *point for mental concentration*. When a person uses his mind to concentrate on an object, a door opens in the spiritual realm and it allows the invocation or worshiping of creatures of any kind. This includes not only divine beings such as gods, angels, saints, virgins, etc., but also spirits or demons.

Practicing all of that is forbidden by the biblical God, even though the person may do it with good intentions. These **<<points>>** of contact may include hundreds of instruments such as images, stamps, statues, figurines, candles, crystals, water, etc. It is clear now, that the Ouija board is included in this long list of things that no one should be using. About this issue, we can read the following:

> *Deuteronomy 5:8-9. 'You* ***MUST NOT MAKE*** *any* ***IDOLS****. Don't make any* ***STATUES*** *or* ***PICTURES*** *of anything up in the sky or of anything on the earth or of anything down in the water.* ***DON'T WORSHIP*** *or serve* ***IDOLS*** *of any kind…*

In a similar way, I must add that many times these objects – even though they have been used for only a single time – remain permanently **<<active>>**. Here, with the word *active* I mean open, and these open instruments can create an untold number of problems for their clueless owners. What happen here is that beings from the spiritual dimension can come and go at will through these open portals. And in general, these types of entities are up to no good most of the times. The aftermath is that the confused owners of these active artifacts cannot determine what is causing them so many adversities in their lives, in their families, and even in their own homes.

Regarding this issue, the Bible teaches that the only point of spiritual contact with God is the Christ himself, and that there are no additional mediators. This information can be read here:

> *1 Timothy 2:5. There is only one God, and there is* ***ONLY ONE WAY*** *that people can* ***REACH GOD. THAT WAY IS*** *through* ***CHRIST JESUS****…*

PSYCHOLOGY OF CHILD 9-10

At this stage in the life of a normal child, the minor is still very dependent on Mom and Dad. The little one seeks after the security offered by his parents and also after the example that they provide. I remember that at this age, I made my mother very angry at me and she banished me from home. That is why, I left my house with no intention to return. During the day, I spent my time bumming around the street. The problem came with the night, as I had no place where I could go to sleep. Since I had no money to pay for a hotel, I hid inside a supermarket chain called *Storehouse Aurrera*. When the store closed, I kept hidden inside. However, this adventure did not last long. In the early morning, I was captured by the security guard, who handed me over to the manager, who luckily made the decision to call my parents instead of the police. My parents picked me up at seven a.m., and I returned home— punished and without eating.

About the Ouija board and the strange phenomenon that it exhibits, psychology offers an explanation in the form of the so-called *ideomotor* effect. According to this effect, the player fools himself by producing unconscious muscular movements. A few investigators explain that most of the reported paranormal occurrences can be explained by this effect itself.

CHAPTER 6
MY DEFIANCE OF SATAN

Nothing memorable happened at my eleven years of age. Nonetheless, because of something shameful I did, now my brother *Gabriel* has a scar on his right arm. What happened is that during one of our daily fistfights, I pushed my brother against a window, and the glass broke and cut his right elbow. My brother had to get several stitches at a hospital to help close the wound. That very same year, my brother took revenge on me. One day he ran me over with his bicycle, and I fell, hitting the floor first with my left elbow. This caused my skin to burst open for about two inches long. The wound was so deep that it was possible to see the bone. Nowadays, my brother has a scar on his right elbow, while I have a scar on the elbow of my left arm.

When I reached twelve years of age, something I remember very well is that I felt completely invincible. That is because I kept thinking that I was smarter, stronger, and faster than any other child my age.

My life was full of contradictions at this age of twelve. My hair had always been straight, and that bothered me. Thus, I used to go to the styling salon to get a perm so that I would have wavy hair. Back then, I had a friend named *Louis*, and he had a naturally curly hair, however, he was not happy about that. Therefore, at the same time I was getting my hair permed, my friend *Louis* was visiting the beauty salon to have his hair straightened. Cheers to being young! Everything seemed upside down. So much contradiction exists in human nature itself. Be that as it may, the <<incoherencies>> of my life did not stop there. Even though I had already encountered many spiritual experiences, I was still skeptical about the existence of God. And, of course, that I did not believe in the existence of Satan, either. In a way, I was worse than the Apostle Thomas in the biblical account. Let's go back a little and try to remember the story told in John chapter twenty, with lines 24 to 28. Here, several disciples who had seen that Jesus had risen, were testifying everywhere. One of those persons they testified to was the Apostle Thomas. Regardless, Thomas argued with them while asking for proof. When they could not provide more evidence than their own testimony, Thomas did **<<not>>** believe in Christ's resurrection and said:

—That's hard to believe. I will have to see the nail holes in his hands, put my finger where the nails were... Only then I will believe it.

The Apostle Thomas came to believe in the resurrection of Christ only when, after a week, when Jesus himself appeared to him in person. Only after that the disciple became a true believer. Although, I dare to say that I was worse than the disciple Thomas of that time because I was seeing many supernatural things, but not even seeing those things could make a believer out of me. And in the absurdity of my ignorance and without having any respect for the spiritual realm, I did something extremely crazy that brought many problems and unbelievable physical pain into my life for several years afterwards. This is what happened…

One good day I was reading the Bible when I realized that Satan was the one who was causing so much turmoil and devastation on Earth. For the sacred scripture says that the *thief* (*Satan*) came to steal, to kill, and to destroy.

Jesus Christ is the one who says all of those things in representation of Lucifer. This can be read in John chapter ten, with verse ten. In the same way, we are warned in the following citation:

> *1 Peter 5:8. Control yourselves and be careful!* ***THE DEVIL IS YOUR ENEMY****, and he goes around like a roaring lion looking for someone to attack and eat.*

When I read such things, it made very angry to know that Satan was the malignant being who pursued, harassed, and destroyed humanity into pieces. Because of that, an **<<brilliant>>** idea occurred to me…

I would challenge Lucifer to a fight. After all, was I not invincible?

On the other hand, in reality, I did not believe in the existence of the Prince of Darkness. Yet, in the remote possibility that this being actually existed, of course, deep inside me, I thought that Satan would never respond to my childish provocations to a fight. In any case, I began to invoke the Devil to defy him.

That was something I enjoyed doing, since it made me feel like an all-great Mexican macho man.

I can only imagine that the increase of the hormone testosterone in my body at that particular time in my life, as well as my constant fights with other young people my age, prompted me to do something foolish. I felt like a super-human, therefore I decided that if Satan was the one to blame for the misfortunes that afflicts humankind day after day, I had the responsibility to teach him a lesson. And following this train of thought, I decided to summon Lucifer. Therefore, this is what I did. Every day and when the clock pointed at twelve o'clock midnight, I stood in the middle of my room and pronounced the following conjure:

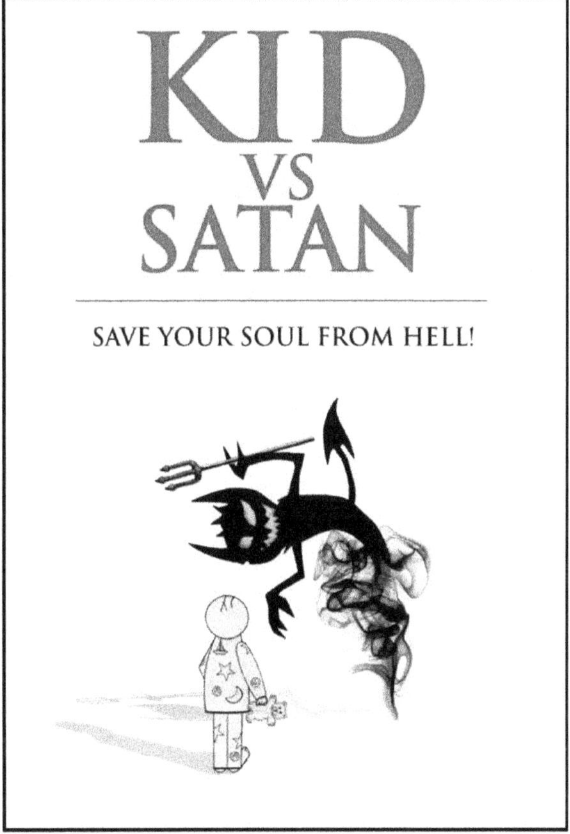
KID
VS
SATAN
SAVE YOUR SOUL FROM HELL!

—Satan, I challenge you to a fight because of the damage you cause to humans!

—You are a thief and a deceiver!

—You are a coward because you do not show yourself!

—Come and face me!

—Come, I will hit you, and you will leave defeated!

I repeated this challenge to the devil every day at midnight, and I did so for around three consecutive years. At this age, I had joined a gym and I was also taking karate classes because, according to me, I believed had to prepare for my big fight against Lucifer. Well, it is clear that any man who challenges the Prince of Darkness to a fight would also train in martial arts. Or would he not? Or was there some other way?

After all, that was my way of thinking at twelve years old, anyways.

PSYCHOLOGY OF CHILD 10-12

From the ages of ten to twelve years old, the little boy is in the age of pre-adolescence. Here, the minor tends to be more independent from his parents, so he need less affection and support from them— at least this is what the kid believes. In the child's effort to become more independent, the relationship between parents and their offspring can change.

In his social interactions with other youngsters, the little one can become competitive, and may try to prove who the best among them is. This could be the reason why the lad, at this age, likes to be more involved in sports and to compete to win. From the twelve years of age and onwards, the time comes in which the growing person tries to see what his physical limits are. That is why the individual continually test himself. Many psychologists explain that this behavior is due to the hormonal changes that the person experiences during these years of maturation. This is the time when the hormones start to work, changing the child, and begin turning him into a teenager.

The above description explains in a very accurate way my behavior at this phase of my life.

THE MYSTERIOUS SHIP

My twelve years of age went by without much more novelty, but when I reached the age of thirteen, I saw something that truly shocked me. It happened that for a weekend on the warm autumn's days, a friend and I visited my grandmother whose name was *Trinidad*. She used to live in a city named *Eye of Water*, in the State of Mexico. Having already passed the weekend with my grandmother, we were already on our way back home to Mexico City. It was a Sunday evening at around eight p.m. At that hour, it was already night and it was dark outside. On our way in car, and just a couple of minutes before arriving in the capital, I saw a ship in the sky. But I am not talking about a simple and common airplane. This vessel had ginormous dimensions. It was like an entire city in the sky. The airship was so gigantic that it had to average at least five hundred miles in circumference. The shape of the ship was like a Frisbee disk. It was circular, and somewhat flattened. Countless of small colored lights – red, yellow, green and blue – surrounded the circumference of the great disk, all along its edge. Its lights turned on and off in sequence just as a Christmas tree lights do.

This formidable flying object was static, and it was not flying directly over the capital, but it was stationed next to it, by the edge of the metropolis. The ship was located near the entrance to the City of Mexico, along a highway road named Towards Pachuca (this area is more commonly known with the name of The Green Indians because of some statues located there).

The great disk was not flying directly over the highway, either. Instead, it was keeping itself to the left, out of sight of the main traffic on the road.

When I saw this object, it astonished me very much. I felt shivers immediately running down from my head to my toes. The truth is, I immediately imagined the worst-case scenario – an extraterrestrial alien invasion.

In my mind, I thought that by the time I made it home, I would find a lot of dead people. Since, I imagined seeing tiny Martians wearing tight silver spacesuits and firing their laser guns merciless from left to right. Right away, I envisioned humanity been **<<enslaved>>** by a superior extraterrestrial race.

For all intents and purposes, I really expected the worst misery possible. At that moment, I thought to myself:

–Did not people kept saying that the flying saucers do not exist?

–Now they have attacked us and we were not ready!

Considering that the airship made no sound or any movement at all, my friend *Isidro*, who was with me at that time, had not notice it. Besides, the flying machine was not directly in front of us, nor was it in our line of sight. If I take, for example, the hour hand of a clock, and if the twelve hour is at the front, then the nine hour would be ninety degrees to the left. That is where the ship was located, at nine o'clock.

Because of my feeling of astonishment at seeing this flying saucer, I could not talk. However, I decided to let my friend know about it. Hence, I hit his left side twice with my right elbow to attract his attention right away. When my friend turned his head, I pointed with my index finger to the sky and to the huge vessel. My friend, while quickly noticing the immense object suspended in the air, became speechless from amazement as well. But he made a short exclamation of **<<Ah!>>** from fright, and with good reason. Upon arriving home, we rushed to the top of a building to see if we could find the magnificent flying disk again. Notwithstanding, our efforts were futile. The object was not visible to the sight from our location or it had simply vanished and was not there anymore. That night we paid much attention to the news on television to see if there was some report on the huge saucer. Nevertheless, there was no mention of it in any news media. But since then something happened in me...

Because ever since I saw that colossal vessel in the air, I became much more interested in science and technology than in finding out if God really existed. I began to place more importance on Darwin's theory of evolution and to the possible existence of intelligent beings in other worlds. And when before that event happened in my life, I really did not care much about school, after that event I took great interest in reading books, and in learning, and in studying. My hunger for knowledge and wisdom keeps on going to this day.

Just about six hundred years ago, the **<<vain>>** human being thought that the Earth was the center of the Cosmos (*with the named Geocentric Theory*). In the same way, just about five hundred years ago, men thought that the Earth was flat. And he who dared to think differently, and did not changed his opinion was burned alive by the political-religious regime of that time.

The current topic in our days is the belief that we are completely <<alone>> as a unique creation of God in the uncountable millions of planets that exist in outer space. That is why, I keep asking myself:

—Why do we humans strive so hard to always keep such a narrow mind?

For that reason, I dare to say that it looks like <<modern>> man is not in any way better than our fellow men from the past.

No matter that we are in the straight out 21st century (XXI), human beings are still wearing – *the same old mantle of arrogance* – that they wore hundreds of years ago. By doing this, man himself has impeded the growth and maturity of the **<<entire>>** human race. In general, the human being of today continues to ridicule the ideas that invite him to think far beyond his comfort zone.

In reality, nothing has changed. The same machinery of punishment and oppression that was used hundreds of years ago is still active in our present-day. The one who dares to say publicly that he believes that there are intelligent beings in other worlds is deemed as a lunatic. And the social system of chastisement comes into action once again. The individual who make the claim to have seeing an unidentified flying object or, going even beyond that, and claim to have had a close encounter with an extraterrestrial being, is not burned alive – but that is nearly what happens.

The unfortunate individual may be fired from his job. He may be expelled from school. He may lose the acceptance of the church he attends, and very often, it may go as far as even losing his friends. The zeal to follow the standards set by society and culture grows to such an extent that the unfortunate person, even in his own home and among his own family, may be seen as a stranger.

Despite of all that, this book will not deal with the subject of unidentified flying objects, either. Although, it is interesting to note that there are important biblical characters who have described seeing odd things flying through the skies and looking like **<<ships>>** or methods of transport. As an example of this, the Bible reports the appearance of a *chariot of fire* flying in the air, with the subsequent disappearance of the Prophet Elijah. Since, at that moment, the famous oracle seemed to have been carried away into the sky by some strange flying object and even though some people went looking for him, they could not find him. His disciple Elisha witnessed this fact, and that is how it is told in the biblical story found in the second book of Kings 2:11.

PSYCHOLOGY OF CHILD 13-14

From the age of thirteen, the child enters the stage of becoming an adolescent. During this period, the young man starts to question authority, popular beliefs, and the values of the society around him. And that was really my condition and situation at that age. My philosophy and mantra during this period of life was:

—*Do not believe in anything, it is better to question everything.*

CHAPTER 7 YOUNG

A MIRACLE HAPPENS

I was fourteen years old of age when my family received the bad news that an aunt of mine, whose name is *Rose,* was very sick. At that time, she lived in the United States, in the state of Illinois. Unfortunately, the doctors had no cures to her afflictions, and some doctors were giving her only a few more months to live.

Back then, a Christian couple spoke to my aunt *Rose* about a Jesus Christ who forgave sins, and who miraculously **<<healed>>** the sick. Afterwards, the Christian couple invited my aunt *Rose* to attend their church. When she arrived at their church, she met the pastors and told them that she was very sick, and the pastors invited her to accept Jesus as her own personal Savior. Luckily, my aunt accepted. After that, the pastors started to pray for her healing, and the surprise was that my aunt *Rose* was healed miraculously at that very instant. As the days passed, she regained her strength, and her weeping, and mourning turned into happiness.

Jumping for joy, she soon began evangelizing the whole family, and that same year my aunt visited Mexico. When she visited my house in Mexico City, my aunt told us about the miracle of her healing performed by Jesus Christ, and she made us visit a Christian church. She vibrated with excitement and she succeeded in spreading to my family her new faith in Jesus. My parents, siblings, and this writer accepted Christ as our Savior in our very first visit to church. Back then, in my opinion, I had become a Christian. However, for me, it was just like the latest fad coming from the United States. My conversion had not been real, as I continued to be as rude and as impertinent as ever. The miraculous healing of my aunt *Rose* had only served to cause me some simply curiosity.

PSYCHOLOGY OF YOUNG 14-15

At this age I tried to avoid contact with my parents as much as I could. To do that, I spent as much time away from home as possible. Basically, I went home only to eat and to sleep. I was very impulsive and I became very interested in playing sports. When I played sports, I could make quick decisions, then back those decisions with actions and with violence. In the mornings, I visited the gym. In the afternoons, I attended school, and after school I played football soccer on the streets at night.

THE REPLY FROM SATAN

By now I was fifteen years old. It had been already three years since I had begun challenging the Devil, and I was still calling upon him to fight every single night. Nevertheless, one day the unexpected happened because Satan answered to my challenge. Lamentably, Lucifer himself did not respond.

For the reason that it seemed that he was engaged in some other endeavor (only God can be everywhere at the same time for he is omnipresent, while the Devil does not have such ability).

Therefore, since Satan was busy with another undertaking, he sent one of his creatures of the underworld to answer to my invocations to a fight. However, apparently, the only demon that was available at the hand of the Prince of Darkness at that moment was an extremely ugly, deformed, and tiny being. Taking into account that the small creature that attacked me was a mere two feet tall.

This amazing experience happened one day when I was at the gymnasium taking karate classes. At that time, I was attending a health club that was several stories high.

This sports center was a huge building that provided all kinds of professional athletic education within it.

After practicing karate, my routine was to go to the fourth floor, where there was a basketball court with a hard, wooden finish. There, I used to spend about an hour throwing the ball through the basketball hoop. It was about 11:30 in the morning, and I was alone. I was still entertained, practicing this activity, when suddenly I noticed something very peculiar.

I was able to discover a dense smoke that seemed to be forming while coming out of the wall in front of me. The color of the wall was of a light beige, and the smoke that was forming was of a very dark gray color, almost swinging to black. Therefore, the bizarre apparition had enough contrast with the background. A slight unpleasant smell of burning plastic filled the atmosphere of the place. For a moment, I considered that the health club had caught on fire. However, nothing made sense because I could not see any fire or flame on the wall, and the fire safety alarm was not making any sound. Furthermore, the building in which I stood was made of very thick concrete walls. When the smoke finally finished coming in, it started to compress and to form a dense fog that flew over the ground. Soon after, the dark and heavy haze started to sail…, slowly and heavily…, towards me… (?).

I paid even more attention to it, and, indeed, I saw the smoke moving towards where I was standing. It seemed like the fog knew about my presence. Intrigued, I looked at it, not knowing what to make of it. As it drew closer and closer to me, I began to realize that something was moving in the interior of the silent and darkened gray cloud.

Within the smoke, I thought I could distinguish a silhouette. Or, rather, was the smoke becoming a humanoid figurine? I did not like that at all, but I did not know how to interpret it either. Everything was so strange. What was it? And great was my surprise when I finally realized that…

It was a demon! I saw a macabre creature pulsing and moving inside the dense and dark fog! The being completely materialized in front of my eyes when he was just about three feet from where I was standing.

This creature had an enormous head that was disproportionate in size in relation to his skinny, naked, and emaciated body. His ovate head was completely bald and it was ten times larger than his body. The creature had pointed ears, just like the ears of a vampire. His eyes were of an impenetrable black color, and they were large and round. Lacking eyelashes and eyelids, his eyes looked permanently open – *and just like the dead eyes of a shark*– his eyes did not seem to emit feelings or any other sign of life.

His nose was not prominent. It was rather flat and level with his facial surface located a bit above the upper middle part of his lip (*lip-philtrum*). His nose consisted of only two small circular holes.

His mouth was completely abnormal, for the banks of the mouth (*oral commissures*) reached literally from ear to ear. And, in this way, his mouth assumed an impossible yet very large smile that exhibited a permanently **<<sarcastic>>** gesture.

The creature had long, thin arms that extended past his waist and knees, reaching as far as his feet. Both of his legs and feet were like the legs and feet of a frog. What surprised me the most about this being were his hands, and more especially his fingers, because his fingers had some very peculiar nails. Every one of his fingernails were ten inches long, and they all looked dangerously pointed and sharp as razor blades. Instead of skin, the entity seemed to have scales like those of a fish or a snake. And his whole body was the same color as the smoke from which he had come from, a very dark gray.

When the demon came closer to me, I was stupefied and slow to react, since I still could not conceive of what I had in front of me. Nevertheless, after a couple of seconds passed, I was able to react, and the first thing I did was to throw towards him the basketball I held in my hands.

However, the ball of basketball simply went through the demon, passing through the upper half of his body. My sudden attack move had not worked. The being did not even blink, nor did he even move to the side. It was as if I had done absolutely nothing.

The creature continued slowly advancing towards me…

But suddenly, as if changing his mind, the evil spirit briefly made a pause and then stopped. Next, the demon began to fly slowly and without any rush around my body, at the height of my eyes. It was as if he was inspecting me or studying me in a very careful manner.

It seemed to me as if, at that precise moment, the demon was analyzing the following question in his huge oviform head:

—Who is this guy who every day dares to challenge my master Satan?

And after making several turns around me — and seeming to have satisfied his curiosity — the entity stopped in the middle of the air and proceeded to stand in front me as in a combat position. The little devil raised his lanky arms, which had been resting at his side, and showed me his palms. He clenched his fists and with a gesture to fight, he challenged me. His smile, incredible long and mocking, never left his face, not even for a second — and as if it was possible it seemed to me that it lengthened even a bit further.

I did not know what to think. Perplexed, I could not guess correctly how to respond or recognize the situation. At that precise moment, I stood speechless and paralyzed. The day of the great fight against Satan had come, and I in my amazement, could not believe it. Even though the Prince of Darkness had not arrived, I certainly had now before me one of his emissaries from the underworld.

Nonetheless, by pure force of habit, I could not believe it, not even while I was seeing it with my very own eyes.

The little demon started advancing towards me, almost without any speed, as if he were the owner and master of time. Instinctively, I lifted and extended both of my arms in front of me, as if to prevent him from getting closer to me. With both arms outstretched and with the palms of my hands, I signaled for him to **<<stop>>**. Although, doing that was useless.

The demon, as if he were actually made of pure smoke, passed the totality of my hands and arms. And when he reached my abdomen, he made several furious swipes with his sharp claws towards my stomach – *just as a tiger does while ripping its prey.* His quick and accurate blows were impossible to dodge.

After attacking me, the entity crossed through me as if I were nothing. The malevolent spirit entered my chest, traversing me and coming out through my back.

When I turned my face around to follow his tracks, I saw him continue to fly with the same calmness and heaviness with which he had arrived. Then he ended up vanishing through the same wall from which he had come from.

I was not sure what had just happened. Though, I decided that I should not pay too much attention to it. For that reason, I decided to forget everything right there. After all, the fierce hunger I was feeling after exercising was playing tricks on me. This had been only an illusion. Right? I had to believe this so in order to preserve my inner peace and to avoid suffering from an anxiety attack. Anyhow, the pain I was feeling at that moment in the intestines of my abdominal region was so great that I thought I was going to fall unconscious. I started walking in a hunched position, looking for the exit of the building. At the same time, I was using my forearms and my hands to put pressure on my stomach, for I felt that I had literally being stabbed. And as well I could, I started a clumsy, wobbly, and sorrowful trip back home. When I finally made it back, I threw myself on my bed. Lying there in a curled-up fetal position, I tried to lessen the terrible pain in my abdomen. Tears were coming from my eyes. My suffering was so brutal that I really wished to die rather than live. I slept the rest of the day and throughout the night. The pain was so excruciating that I thought I would not live to see the light of a new rising sun…

But the morning came and I was still alive. Although, after that my life changed completely. For I never got to be the athletic guy I was before because now I walked slightly stooped.

If I was lying in bed, to get up I had to do it little by little or the pain appeared again. Even to go to the bathroom to pee, I had to seat on the toilet, for if I did not do that, the pain in my intestines became unbearable. Nor could I lift anything heavy with my arms and hands anymore, for if I exerted even a minimal effort, the *merciless* pain would become present again.

Sometimes, while walking, I had a great stabbing pain in my stomach. The pain was so acute that wherever I was, I immediately had to throw myself onto the floor. Once on the floor, I would put myself into the fetal position to ease the discomfort, and I would remain lying there for several minutes until the torment had passed. I was left crippled.

Notwithstanding, as time went on I got used to my new life of suffering. As a curious fact, the Apostle Paul speaks of a **<<thorn>>** stuck in his body, which, as an instrument of Satan, was used to mistreat and cause suffering in his life. This can be found in the second letter to the Corinthians, chapter twelve. Apparently, this was allowed by God so that Brother Paul would not have a higher concept of himself. In other worlds, to keep him humble, being that the Celestial Father used him to do great miracles.

Sometimes I think that I understand what Saint Paul wrote, for my pains appeared all of a sudden, like a real sting. It was as if suddenly *something* was pulling my navel from inside me. However, far from being humble and seeking God, I never acknowledged my need or my poor state of someone who needed help— a miserable lost soul. And probably, because of the same opposition existing in the self-centered human nature, I finished rebelling myself, so I did exactly the opposite. I hid behind vainglory, and my mind formed a protective, arrogant, and vain barrier around me. The Divine Father knows too well that human beings are not physically prepared to wage war against the devil. If someone wants to battle Satan, the individual can, but not alone. Given that it is with the help of God himself, and it is with the aid of his **<<Holy Spirit>>**. And you will be glad to know that He is more than willing to help you fight. But, to fight against Lucifer and his falling angels, a person has to be covered first with the *Holy Spirit*. That is why it is written as follows:

> *Zechariah 4:6. He said, "This is the message from the Lord to Zerubbabel: 'Your help will not come from your own strength and power. No, your* **HELP WILL COME FROM MY SPIRIT.**' *This is what the Lord All-Powerful says.*

PSYCHOLOGY OF YOUNG 15-16

Egocentrism or narcissism may affect this stage of the adolescence. Both words mean an exaggerated exaltation of the personality. And although egocentrism and narcissism are similar concepts, in the end they each assume a different meaning. An egocentric needs the acceptance and admiration from those around him, while a narcissist does not demand approval from anybody. It is also said that egocentrism is a little more innocent than narcissism, for an egocentric does not know how to understand those around him, while a narcissistic simply does not care.

An egocentric or narcissistic teenager possibly occupies himself excessively on how he looks in front of a mirror. He can even come to believe that he is superior to others. The young may manage to think that his ideas, interests and needs are better and more important than those of his family, friends or classmates. Therefore, his priorities are ahead everybody else's. At that age, I was a narcissist. I believed I was more capable and more important than other people, without requiring the consent of anyone. That was exactly my indigent way of conduct and way of thought at this age. My mantra and philosophy at this stage of life was: *Every second of my life, I die a little.* Because I began to reconsider my own mortality and I stopped believing that I was invulnerable.

WHY NOT TO BELIEVE IN GOD?

It did not take long for me to reach sixteen years of age. However, even though I had already experienced various types of suffering, my heart hardened once again. Far from accepting the idea that there was an Omnipotent God, I rejected his possible existence. So, I told myself the following:

—The strange stuff that I have saw and lived never occurred because it is simply impossible.

This remind me of what it is said to have happened to the Pharaoh of Egypt something more than 4000 years ago. Because the Pharaoh, even after seeing the miracles and wonders from God, hardened his heart and suffered with all of his people by refusing to believe. His own magicians and diviners informed him:

—This is hand and work of God.

But the King of Egypt would not yield. This story can be read in the book of Exodus, chapters from five to twelve. In my case, instead of seeking God, at that age I thought I was a god, owner and master of my life. Despite of all the problems I already had, I filled myself with pride. I became a bit more atheistic and unbelieving of what I already was. Then, I wrapped up myself and hid in theories explaining why not to believe in God. Let's see now, as an atheist, what did I believe in?

An atheist can believe in Mother Nature, evolution, and science as a perfect explanation of everything that exists. By not loving the Father Creator, I loved myself exclusively. Only I existed. I was first, I was afterwards, and I was last. It was too hard for me to believe that there was a supreme being that could do everything and that was eternal. Besides, if it was true that there existed such a *formidable* being..., how was it possible that good and innocent people suffered so much in this world? I thought that a good and benevolent God would not let so many bad things happen. If the Father of the Heavens actually existed, then why did he allow pain and suffering? And the answer to those questions was easy, well, what happens is that... God does not exist. From a medical and scientific point of view, the birth of Jesus of Nazareth to a virgin woman was impossible. In the same way, his alleged miracles could not be confirmed. And how to verify the resurrection of Jesus? The whole history of Christ was simply absurd. Thus, the answer to the existence to the Jewish Messiah was easy too, well, what happens is that... Jesus does not exist. *It is a mere fantasy tale,* I told myself.

Sometimes I used to think about all the religions and the problem of having so many religious denominations. This made it difficult to accredit any religion or denomination as the true bearer of the divine message.

Afterwards the question became, Why be a Catholic and not a Christian? Or, why no to profess Judaism or Buddhism? Why no to follow Islamism or Hinduism? And the list of questions continued without stopping. In the end, the answer was simple, and each time I reached the same conclusion. Well, what happens is that simply... God does not exist. If God were real – *surely he would not allow this much confusion* – I analyzed.

Studying a few different religions, I realized that each one of them was incompatible with the others. This contrariety among them is what gives a distinctive and singular nature to each one of them, and it is this same incompatibility that helps to create different religions. Nevertheless, because of the aforementioned, not all religions can be correct, although **<<all>>** of them can be wrong... Those were my final deductions.

Still, someone would dare to say that any religion leads to God, in one way or another. However, such assertion would be quite improbable because many of those religions even have different gods.

Following this line of questioning, then the next question to ask was, who is the real God? Or, which ones are the true gods? Should I believe in one and unique God and in monotheism? Or, should I believe in the existence of multiple gods and in polytheism?

I also began to question the origin of the Bible. Who wrote that book, God or man? Of course, man did, and throughout the course of thousands of years. And for what real purpose was it written? Of course, to instill fear and to gain control over the population. And the same ideology could be applied to the sacred books of all the other religions.

Already thinking about other types of reasoning to seek God, I was left with the – *scientific method* – which had been presented to me in graduate school. This teaches how to probe the veracity of things through repetitive, measurable, and reliable experiments. It is necessary for me to add that the scientific method will never help anybody to find God, because God is love and the given method is incapable to study or to measure love (*see 1 John 4:8*).

Someday, science and technology could agree and share with the public, that there are enough clues to deduce that God exists. But then it would be doubtful that science and technology could help mankind to establish a personal relationship with the Heavenly Father, for the reason that this is simply not God's plan for the moment. I say this because, according to the Bible, God has already prepared a very specific way for human beings to encounter him. It is like one of those secrets that hide in plain sight, right in front of everyone, and I that will gladly reveal in a later chapter.

CHAPTER 8
ADULT
ROCK & ROLL

My family had moved to the country of the United States of America, while I had stayed behind in Mexico. Though, shortly after that I followed them and moved back in with my parents. Now I was already seventeen years old, and I was completely passionate about music. Especially rock music. Its sounds, videos, fashion, showbiz, and celebrities all fascinated me. I dreamed of becoming a member of a rock music band. Therefore, I devoted all of my time to learn music and to play the guitar. I was taking music lessons in the afternoons, while at night I played guitar in my house until dawn. That is how my days from 17 to 19 years of age went by, and with peers I met in music school, we formed a band. For the first time in my life, I thought I was happy. The music helped me to ignore my inner pain and gave a purpose to my life. In addition, with the musical project I could forget the emptiness I felt in my chest and in my life. I was excited and I really imagined that my future would be dedicated to playing rock music forever. Back then I had dreams of greatness, fame, and fortune just like many young people do at that age.

But one of those days, the sad news that my cousin *Theresa's* health had turn for the worse reached the ears of my family all the way to the USA. Her seizures were increasing in number every day, and she was becoming more aggressive each time. We were told that one day *Theresa* had become violent and had beaten people who had tried to take her into a church. We also heard that her mother *Hortensia* was desperate to help her, and my aunt was willing to send her daughter to the USA. At that moment, the plan to send my cousin to the USA stemmed from the fact that my aunt *Rose* had married an American pastor named *Mike*. And Pastor *Mike* and my aunt *Rose* had raised a church that already served a congregation of about twenty-five people. The idea developed by my aunt *Hortensia* was that she wanted Pastor *Mike* to be in charge of carrying out an **<<exorcism>>** or as the Christian Church calls it– *a liberation* – for my cousin. The exorcism of *Theresa* had already been attempted in some churches in Mexico, but nothing seemed to work. Upon hearing the news that Theresa's health had gotten worse, I got saddened because I remembered that we used to play together when we were kids. In a way, I was glad when all the people involved in my aunt *Hortensia's* plan agreed to help. By that, I mean that my mother *Mary of Socorro*, my aunt *Rose*, and the Pastor *Mike* agreed to bring *Theresa* to the USA.

They acted quickly, and in matter of a couple of weeks my mother traveled to Mexico to pick up *Theresa* to then take her to the home of my aunt *Rose* and Pastor *Mike*.

By that time my aunt *Rose* had moved several years previously to a town named Rancho Cucamonga, in California. My aunt *Rose* lives in that city to this day and that is where my cousin *Theresa* arrived. After she went through a couple of months of being – bored to death – with counseling and praying, *Theresa* said that she was feeling better, and that she wanted to return to Mexico as soon as possible. She said goodbye to Pastor *Mike* and to Aunt *Rose*, then went to live with my family for a few days before her trip back to Mexico.

Nevertheless, the hope that everybody had – that Pastor Mike had helped Theresa to recover her health – simply crumble to the ground, as *Theresa* began to pass out in my house.

As a good atheist, I was greatly disappointed in Pastor *Mike*. Therefore, I thought to myself:

–Pastor Mike, where is your God?

–It is clear, of course that God does not exists!

I internally mocked the idea.

But now I know that it was all a plan drawn up by the divinity itself. That is because right when there seemed to be no hope, everything started to work for the good. And this is what happened…

My cousin *Theresa* came to live with my family, which at that time was located in the city of Santa Ana, in California. In those days, *Theresa* loved to exercise, as she had always been a very active person. One day, with the idea of playing sports, she went to the park that was right across of the street from where we lived. There in that place, she met a guy named *Xavier*.

This man looked exceedingly strange. He had a military-style haircut, with the top flat and the sides clipped very short. He wore sunglasses, cargo pants, and combat boots. On his neck he wore a cheap stainless steel ball chain from which hung a perforated copper bullet. He wore a black leather jacket that reached to his knees. An old book with a wine-colored cover, pale and worn by the use and the time, rested under one of his arms, finishing off his attire.

His language and his accent were equally unusual to me. For he is a native of the city of Usulutan, from the country of El Salvador, and the Spanish language changes somewhat, since it is not the same as the Mexican Spanish. Many words change, a Mexican word may have a different meaning in the country of El Salvador, and vice-versa. Nonetheless, *Xavier,* falling in love at the first sight with *Theresa,* began to visit her in my house. *Xavier* not only looked like an out-of-the ordinary character, along with that he had a story that was even stranger, or rather, I would say **<<exotic>>**.

He described having had a very sad and extremely poor childhood. He had been part of the army in his country, and had taken part in the conflict against the guerilla warfare years ago. So he said, he had been a military man. After the war ended, he decided one day to leave his native country and move to the USA. Then he narrated that after reaching the USA, he visited a church, where he accepted Jesus as his Lord and Savior. But shortly afterward, disillusioned with the hypocrisy of some very unspiritual members, he decided to put aside the church matter and went to work in various illicit businesses.

He said that through those dealings he had achieved success, and that he handled thousands of dollars' worth of money. However, his best friend had become envious of his success and had betrayed him. *Xavier* detailed to us that just a few months previously, the so-called best friend had fired at him twice with a twenty-two-caliber pistol at point blank range, in order to take his money and his position in the business. *Xavier* showed us the two recent gunshot wounds on his chest, one close to the heart and the other one by the area of the lungs. He showed us his wounds because he wanted us to believe him, so we could verify his story.

After receiving the shots, he told us that an ambulance had picked him up, and that by the time he arrived at the hospital, he saw himself coming out of his body since he had already died.

Xavier said that when he came out of his body, he remained hovering right above his bloody corpse, saying:

—Look, poor little man, the way he looks, his face seems so sad…

He also commented that while he watched this scene, which lasted until he arrived at the operating room of the clinic, a shiny light appeared to him and that he was heading towards that light. Subsequently, he added that a voice came out of that light, and said to him:

—You cannot come to me yet. Return to your body. You have to preach my word. Tell everybody that I am Jesus Christ, and that my kingdom is real and truthful.

—Tell them that **<<I>>** *will come soon for a church that is clean and honest.*

Under those circumstances, *Xavier* was sent back to his body, and in the hospital he was revived by artificial methods. When his life was already out of danger in the sanatorium, he said that he was sent to prison. And that after he had been in jail for not very long, he had been allowed to leave without any criminal charges being filed against him. According to *Xavier,* he was now alive and a free man, only to devote himself to preach the gospel of the Lord Jesus. He asserted that Christ himself had taken care of the speedy recovery of his wounds, and had also taken him promptly from the hospital, and then from the penitentiary.

After telling us his story, *Xavier* invited us to a Christian church, which he regularly attended every week. The name of the church is – *Ray of Light* – and even though it has moved its whereabouts several times, the temple is located to this day in the city of Santa Ana, in California.

As part of my family, I also have a sister whose name is *Veronica.* And my sister *Veronica* and my cousin *Theresa* began to regularly attend the church Ray of Light. Just a few days later, I joined them and also began attending the religious church services there. However, I did so primarily to keep an eye on my sister and on my sick cousin who suffered from fainting, not for any other reason. The story that *Xavier* had told us was interesting. Nevertheless, in my opinion he was just a weird guy, and who knows, for all I knew, maybe he was also mentally ill. I did not trust him. And the bad thing was that now I had him almost daily in my home. In addition, of course I was seeing him at the church all of the time, and each time he saw me at my home or at the church, he never missed the opportunity to repeat the following message:

–*Come to a retreat in the mountains and let's fast to seek the presence of God.*

–*And when we return, you will no longer be the same man.*

At this point, perhaps the reader is wondering, what is a retreat?

A <<retreat>> is a place that is especially and specifically prepared to seek the improvement of the spiritual life of an individual. This is done through fasting, prayer, Bible reading, and fellowship with the brotherhood who has the intention of seeking the same objective. At that moment in my life, I thought I was happy enough with my musical projects, and I was not interested in changing, even in the slightest. To my own judgment and knowledge, I was perfectly fine and did not need anything else. Time passed quickly. The months went by, and now I was already 19 years old. One of those days, *Xavier* extended the same invitation he always did, and I decided to accept. As I thought:

—I will go to the retreat and I will come back being the same person.

—What change is Xavier talking about?

—If I attend the retreat, of course I will come back the same man I have always been.

—I am not going to change, I do not need it.

—And once I show up at the retreat and return the same person, Xavier will no longer bother me anymore with the same issue.

Thus, thinking that I was going to get rid of the annoying *Xavier* and that nothing unusual would happen, I accepted the invitation. Hence, I made plans to go to the retreat along with my sister *Veronica* and my cousin *Theresa.* In a little bit, we would be marching together on a trip to a mysterious adventure...

CHAPTER 9

MOUNT CARMEL

The day to go to the retreat finally arrived. It was a Friday, and it was somewhere around eight o'clock in the evening when we left for the mountains of California. *Xavier* was the designated car driver. The other passengers were my sister *Veronica, Theresa,* and me.

For me, visiting that place was a complete waste of time because I was losing the opportunity to practice with the band, given that we gathered to play on the weekends. For that reason, I was not happy at all. We drove along highways and through long stretches of desolated and shadowy roads. It took us over two hours to bump into the location.

Upon arrival, we saw that the main street where the retreat was located had no pavement, it was all dirt. It had just rained in the mountains and the road was badly eroded. On the street were large ditches caused by the high volume of water that ran down below the path. A compact car like the one we were in had trouble crossing the way, which at that time consisted of pure water and mud.

Xavier crossed the deep holes and elongated trenches very slowly and carefully to prevent the automobile from getting stuck there.

The establishment was located uphill on the banks of a mountain, and at that late hour of the night – everything looked deserted. Far and from some distance away, only the barking of dogs could be heard, which, with their hypersensitive ears, had noticed our arrival. Those dogs did not belong to the retreat, but to the neighbors living in the nearby area.

It was very cold in the mountains. When I talked, I could see my own breath turning into vapor before my face (*fogging*).

The site was enclosed by an entwined metal fence surrounding the entire rectangular perimeter. Inside of it there were about five mobile homes, or as they are also called, pre-fabricated houses. These were located in different positions within the boundary, thus covering most of the area. These pre-fabricated homes had the distinctive feature of having wheels underneath them to allow for mobility and easy relocation. The location did not make a good impression on me. Anyhow, we had finally reached the retreat named *Mount Carmel* in the nearness to the mountains of San Bernardino, California.

When we arrived there, it was well past ten o'clock at night. *Xavier* got out of the car and removed a chain from the door's gate. After that he slid the **<<heavy>>** metal door that served as the main entrance, and parked the vehicle inside the place.

The plan was for us to stay there for at least a couple of days, and for the weekend. Therefore, each of us carried backpacks. The backpacks contained a change of clothes, and hygiene items such as toothpaste, shampoo, and soap so that we could freshen up during our stay there.

Afterwards, we went into a house that was of a single story, but it was quite spacious. This was the main or principal house, and there we met some people who inspired tenderness as I had never encountered before until that day.

The name of the Pastor was *David,* and his wife's name was *Priscilla.* Both pastors were of a mature adult age. Pastor *David* was sixty-one, and his wife, being two years older than her husband, enjoyed sixty-three years of age at that point in time.

The beautiful pastoral couple treated us as if we were their own family. They made us feel at home immediately and called us brothers. These pastor brothers inspired confidence, respect, and affection.

They were also the best example of spiritual leaders I had ever encountered up to that moment.

That very same night, Pastor *David* recommended me that while I was at the retreat I should be **<<fasting>>**. This was because fasting was used as a form of sacrifice to God within that place.

I told him that I have never fasted, not even for a single day in my life, and that if I felt hunger – for as much as he would become angry at me – I would drive away in the car to the nearest store, looking for something to eat. He agreed. Notwithstanding, Pastor *David* told me that he would pray for me so that I would not feel **<<discomfort>>** while offering the fasting to God. Immediately, the pastor proceeded to lay his hands over my head and made a little prayer. I did not feel anything special during that short prayer, which did not last even a minute.

Afterwards, those who were present began to pray inside the house, although I limited myself to observing with reverence. That night we went to bed at around three-thirty in the morning. We had stayed up late entertaining ourselves by talking with the pastors about the Bible and Jesus Christ. We also talked about how they had come with the idea of settling in that remote corner of the world.

The story they told about the origin of the retreat was difficult for me to believe. They stated that for many years they had been just regular members of a Christian church. Nevertheless, things had changed when God had communicated with them through a series of dreams.

In those visions, the Eternal Father had told them that they had to buy a place in the mountains to establish a spiritual shelter.

Inclusively, in one of the dreams, the vision of the place had appeared along with a complete address of the property they should be interested in buying. After looking for the property, they realized that it actually existed. And, if that was not coincidence enough, it was for sale. However, the establishment was offered for an amount of money they could not afford. Far from being discourage, they spoke with the owners, and told them that they could pay only 85% of the asking price because that was the limit of their bank loan.

David and *Priscilla* communicated to the actual owners that God had told them in a dream that they would be the new owners. They asked the current owners to please accept their offer for the property, even though they could not pay full price for it. At that moment, the owners told them that they had to talk to each other and that they would give them their decision later. After eight days had passed, the couple received the call of acceptance of their offer, and they gladly, and without any delay signed the purchase contracts.

Therefore, after being regular members of a church – they became spiritual pastors of the retreat – of which they themselves baptized with the name of *Mount Carmel*.

And all this was ordained and arranged by none other than by the Creator of Life himself. Or, at least that is what the affectionate and endearing couple narrated.

The next day we got up early at seven in the morning to pray and to read the Bible. I was able to read the sacred book, but about all the other activities I preferred to just observe.

A bit after midday, we met a group of brothers who had come to visit from another church.

It was a group of about nine people who, without losing any time, began singing praises to God.

Inside the main or principal house, there was a room large enough to accommodate somewhere around twenty people. This large room had the function of being a miniature church, and it was completely arranged with a platform, pulpit, musical instruments and chairs. And that was where we all were. Sister *Priscilla* joined us by playing the piano. She enjoyed to sing praise choruses, and she did it with great joy and with passion.

As the evening advanced, somewhere around three-fifteen p.m., some of us went on an excursion to the top of a mountain.

During our ascent, I was able to see great stones and boulders. And we lined up zigzagging between the large rocks, and between one and another green bush.

As I reached a considerable height above the surface, I could see a par of birds flying jovially over the valley, that little by little, was been drawn beneath our feet.

Upon reaching the top, each individual separately engaged in reading the Bible, praying or singing. I even saw one person starting to cry. For my part, I was no longer angry. I even liked what I had experienced so far, for I felt that people were free to express themselves as they wished. I saw no one criticizing anyone else. Each person minded his or her own business and with evident fervor and dedication.

The way I saw it, this was beginning to look like some kind of *group therapy.* In psychology, a therapy group is an association of people who get together to mutually help each other. The main idea of a typical meeting is to allow people to vent their emotions by freely expressing their feelings and their problems. This type of therapy greatly helps the person to know himself and it also helps to improve relations between individuals. Group therapies are known to be quite effective in treating problems of loneliness, depression, anxiety, and addiction. All this guided by a psychotherapist who has the preparation to evaluate and generate changes in behavior, attitude, and ways of reasoning.

Thinking about these things, now I was standing on a large rock at the peak of the mountain.

Downhill, the landscape showed perfectly aligned fields, with a few small houses. I had misjudged, the place was beautiful, and not as forsaken as I had first imagined.

Up there the wind was hitting my face with a moderate force and I breathed some fresh and pure air. I felt a little cold, but I also managed to feel free of everything. I believe that in that place worldly problems became insignificant. Like that, standing at the top, a strange feeling embraced me. I felt as if I was closer to God. Of course, conceding that he existed. There, I pronounce these words:

—God, in reality, I have never search for you as I am doing it today… Do you really exist?

Then, I felt a great desire to open the Bible that I carried with me. Just by opening it, the single pages, as if moved by the air, passed from one to another until the sheets of the book stopped at a specific location. It was in the book of Psalms where a verse stood out among all the other scriptures, as if it were made bright by a small luminosity. And this is what I read:

> *Psalm 84:10.* ***ONE DAY*** *in your Temple is better than a thousand days anywhere else. Serving as a guard at the gate of my God's house is better than living in the homes of the wicked.*

At that moment, reading this citation I understood that all the past days of my life were of no value to God. However, if I sought God for even a single day, that one day **<<truly>>** had a special value for Him.

However, I thought that I had found that scripture by mere coincidence and not by some paranormal activity, since it was quite windy above the rock where I was standing. Coming down from the mountain and returning to the retreat, we went into the main house and sat in the living room, dedicating ourselves to watching videos – about some famous Christian's testimonies. Seeing these videos made a great impact on me because I heard people talking about the wonders that God had done in their lives. We saw testimonies of all kinds of people, of different sexes, ages, educational levels, cultures, and social classes. Those who testified were a former Satanist, a former homosexual, a former drug addict, and a former prostitute.

On one hand, each of these testimonies was different, but on the other hand, they all had something in common. They all talked about what their lives had been like before they meet Jesus, and of course, each of them had a different lifestyle. But what they all had in common is that each of them narrated a personal encounter with the Jewish Messiah with an extreme luxury of details.

By seeing these testimonies, my poor mind, incapable to grasp these concepts, just got filled with questions and prejudices. At that moment, I thought to myself:

—*These people are paid actors!*

—*What are they saying? It cannot be!*

And a gang – *formed by ruthless doubts* – violent and abusive, persecuted me to beat me up without mercy.

On Sunday night at around nine-thirty p.m., we were already on our way back home to the city of Santa Ana. By then, I had forgotten that I had not eaten anything for several hours. Because I was still fasting, I had not eaten food, nor I had drunk water, since the previous Friday night. And it was already Sunday night, Monday was about to arrive.

This was inconceivable to me. Somehow, I had managed to pass forty-eight hours without eating any food and without drinking any water. And as incredible as it was to me, I was still not hungry, nor I was thirsty either. Other than that, I did not feel anything abnormal.

Something else that caught my attention was the way people expressed themselves at the retreat. As the persons there spoke of Jesus as if they were talking of a close friend. People in that place did speak so much about Christ, that a **<<seed>>** had already been planted in my heart.

Inside the automobile, and on our trip back home, I began to question myself...

Looking through the car's window and contemplating the stars, I thought that if God existed, he would be so far away. If God existed, possibly he lived beyond the stars which I could see up there in the darkness of the sleepy, blue, and crystal-clear firmament.

Nevertheless, the persons at the retreat spoke of God as if he were their next-door **<<neighbor>>** or something of the sort. It was extremely strange for me to listen to those people in that place talk that way about a being who was supposed to be the creator of all things made.

Thereupon, I thought that if God did exist…

—Why would he be so interested in such an *infamous* creature as the human being? And in reality, there were no answers. Except that days later, after reading the holy scripture, I saw that in the book of Genesis chapter one, with citations from twenty-six to twenty-seven, man had been created in the image and likeness of God. This can be read in:

> *Genesis 1:27. So God created humans* ***IN HIS OWN IMAGE****. He created them to be like himself. He created them male and female.*

From here, I started to formulate some other ideas…

—If Satan hates God, and cannot overcome Him for it is written that — *the light shines in the darkness, and the darkness has not defeated it* — in John chapter 1:5.

Can it be that…

—The Devil, while being unable to defeat God, then takes revenge on God?

And in order to achieve that, Satan destroys humankind…

—Because in humans, the Devil can see God?

Therefore…

—Could it be that God is interested in human beings because He is defending them from Satan?

If so, then, could it be possible to deduct that…

—Jesus Christ had been sent here to help us?

Absorbed, I kept planting ideas in my head and I meditated on all this. It was a fascinating subject, yet somewhat confusing, tiresome, and abstract. On account that I could only work with ideas and concepts that were vague, imprecise, and highly imaginative.

CHAPTER 10

THE MUSIC GOT DISTORTED

After driving the required more than two hours of travel, we finally reached the city of Santa Ana, and our household. That night I slept with the best disposition for starting my daily routine, as I did every day at sunrise.

At last the morning came. Upon awakening, the first thing I did was to put a disk with some rock music on my music player so that I could start the day with energy. But something very strange happened because the music sounded **<<distorted>>**. Naturally, the first thing I thought was that my sound system had broken. Greatly disappointed, but still eager to start my day the best way possible, I turned on the radio and tuned the dial into a rock station. But, to my great disconcert, the music sounded equally *bad*. The melody, along with the rhythm, and the harmony – the whole thing about the songs seemed wrong.

Everything had an incorrect intonation. The instruments did not appear to accompany each other. Even the voice sounded as if it were singing in slow motion, completely out of tune and indifferent to the other instruments. I tried to play some music on as many electronics as I had at my disposal at that moment. Anyhow, the result was always the same – *the songs sounded ugly and impossible to listen to.*

I got extremely nervous. I started spinning around in my room as if I were a wild animal that had just been captured and caged. In my confused and distressed mind, I tried to find a logical explanation for what had happened to the music, but nothing made sense and I got afraid. I began to develop the idea that maybe being at a very high altitude on the peak of the mountain had somehow affected my ears (*barotrauma*). I also wondered whether I had caught some infection or sickness in my auditory system, so I felt extremely worried. Therefore, I set out to make an appointment with an otolaryngologist (*a doctor who specializes in the ear*) for Tuesday morning. As the hours passed by, stuck in my room, meditating, I began to remember the words that *Xavier* used to say to me all the time:

–*Come to the retreat… You will not be the same…*

I passed all day long inside the house, perplexed, and shocked. It was a Monday in the afternoon.

As at about six-ten p.m., my sister *Veronica* and my cousin *Theresa* asked me if I would attend to the church service that was about to start at seven o'clock in the evening. I said yes, but I in reality, I felt destroyed. I had become a bit melodramatic.

The rock music was my *treasure*, my new toy, and now I no longer had anything for entertainment. I also thought that I now had no longer a future.

Plunged into these thoughts the minutes passed, and at around six-forty p.m., together we headed to the religious reunion. When we got to the church, the worship team had already started, and as I entered the temple, I heard the choirs of praise to God.

To my surprise, the music combined its sounds with perfect timing and pauses. The music *sang poetry* in complete harmony, and bragged about it in front of my face, as when one displays a newly won trophy.

It was as if the angels themselves were singing and playing the instruments. The sound was celestial, it was superhuman.

It was like a masterpiece that a great artist was painting in the air, and only my ears could *see* its greatness.

I felt as if my brain was **<<melting>>** like a wax candle placed in front of a hot wood-burning stove. And so, just like that, I was left open-mouthed over that much beauty.

For a second, I felt ridiculed and clumsy. Yet, the next instant I became amaze and in a **<<marveled>>** state, I accepted it. I had fought the idea for such a long time, but that day I was able to recognize a great and an extraordinary truth... **Yes...** ***God does exist!***

What had happened to me with the music showed me that God had the power to interact and to change the interior of human beings.

And that additionally...

—He was willing to do it!

The idea that the Eternal Father existed, and that at the same time, he was interested in me created hope within my being. And from this experience comes the second step to save your soul...

SECOND STEP TO SAVE THE SOUL

The second step to be saved is – **Have Faith**. In this step, it is necessary to use faith to make an effort to believe that God exists. In the same way, you can also use faith to believe that God wants to make a real and permanent change in you.

Dear reader, do you know what faith is? We could quickly define it as – I do not see it, but I believe it. It is that simple, without the need for complex definitions.

For your soul to be saved, it is extremely necessary to summon the faith found in you. The biblical scriptures that you will read next back me up on what I said:

*Hebrews 11:1. **FAITH** is what **MAKES REAL THE THINGS WE HOPE FOR**. It is proof of what we cannot see.*

*Hebrews 11:6. Without **FAITH** no one can please God. **WHOEVER COMES TO GOD MUST BELIEVE** that he is real and that he rewards those who sincerely try to find him.*

Therefore, have faith and expect only good things. If you have faith, any good desire of your heart has a chance to come true. With faith, there is an opportunity. Without faith, there is a very little chance of something happening because the person does not expect to receive anything at all. Now can you see what a big difference this is? If you expect to receive something grandiose, such as the experience of the salvation of your soul, then seek to have faith. Have the illusion and confidence that you will experience salvation. In this way, I ask you to fight the negative thoughts that keep telling you that God does not exists, that your life will never change, and that you will never experience anything from the Divine Father. The pessimistic type of thinking will not help you achieve this goal. Additionally, it is necessary for you to realize that this is not – *a maybe or a perhaps* – since there is no middle ground in the spiritual realm.

By that I mean that when God manifests in your life, you will know it well. Either you receive it all or you receive nothing, but you will never receive a half of something from God. And if someone lacks faith, it can be obtained according to the Bible, by **<<hearing>>** the word of God. This is how it is written in the book of Romans, chapter ten, with line seventeen.

In my opinion, the easiest way to increase your faith is by listening to the Christian testimonies. As these narrate the – *miracles and wonders* – that God makes day after day in the lives of countless people. And believe me that if you look for it, there is plenty of information you can find in all type of media so that you can hear the word of God. For example, this book, in its Audible Edition, has as one of its objectives to increase your faith.

I especially like listening to Christian testimonies in the website of *www.youtube.com* because that helps me to increase my faith. When you hear the testimonies, and you realize that Jesus is still healing the terminally ill, helping freeing the captive, and raising the dead, your faith will definitely… Grow.

Jesus himself teach us that all things are possible for the person who believes (Mark 9:23). Let's follow his advice!

SEEKING DIVINE HEALING

I give up the rock band because its music had no more meaning for me. Now I was completely entertained with the idea that God actually did exist. At nineteen years of age, I dedicated myself to seeking Jesus as I had never done it before. *Veronica, Theresa, Xavier,* and I were determined to attend the church every service day and to continue visiting the retreat. For me, this opportunity represented a chance to satisfy my curiosity, for I wanted to see what else might happen. Of course, this also became a hope to cure the fainting and other problems that my cousin *Theresa* suffered from. With that purpose in mind, we started attending the Mount Carmel retreat every single weekend.

I could have never imagined what was about to happen to me. I did not know that I was also in desperate need of help. I do not know why, but I could not recognize my own condition of a being who was sick in sin and sentenced to **<<death>>**. Instead, I was only seeking God out of a mere curiosity. I still believed that my way of thinking and acting was fine, and that there was nothing that I had to change about myself. I was unable to recognize my vanity and my misbehavior.

I felt that I was a self-sufficient man. I always believed that I did not need anything or anyone else to achieve my goals.

Notwithstanding, I knew that in my heart I had only <<hatred>> for humans, but I could do nothing to change that. Each time I listened to sermons at church about love for my fellow man, I experienced a lot of confusion. For example, if someone talked about the stated in 1 John 2:11:

> *1 John 2:11. But* **WHOEVER HATES** *their brother or sister is in darkness. They live in darkness. They don't know where they are going, because* **THE DARKNESS HAS MADE THEM BLIND**.

After listening to a preaching from a citation like that one, I thought to myself:

—*If I could take the hatred away from me in the same way I can take off the t-shirt I am wearing, I would.*

—*But I cannot, because hatred is part of me.*

Therefore, irritated, I wondered what people at church were talking about. For the reason that I did not understand the concept of love, my knowledge was blinded to this reality. The messages about affection and brotherhood made me feel as though I really did not belong to the body of Christ, even though now I was attending church every day of service.

The inner hatred that I was feeling towards my neighbor formed a barrier that separated me from the sanctuary of Christ. There are many biblical scriptures that preach about love, but this quote in first of John 3:14, particularly bothered me every time I read it because it showed me how unfortunate my inner reality was.

> *1 John 3:14. We know that we have left death and have come into life. We know this because* ***WE LOVE EACH OTHER*** *as brothers and sisters.* ***ANYONE WHO DOES NOT LOVE IS STILL IN DEATH.***

PSYCHOLOGY OF YOUNG 17-19

At this age of nineteen. I had a disproportionate interest in myself. My self-esteem flew above the outer space, and I would not accept any criticism towards me. I also had an acute disregard to the feelings and problems of others.

CHAPTER 11

THE TRUE CONVERSION

The months passed quickly, and we were still attending the retreat every single weekend, without missing a single time. One of those many Fridays, we were preparing to go to the retreat, as it was now our routine. However, my car broke down that same Friday evening.

I called *Xavier* to give him the bad news that we could not drive my automobile to Mount Carmel, and I asked him if we could take his vehicle on this occasion.

He told me that just a couple of days ago his car had also broken down, and on the grounds of that, he too, had no means of transportation at that moment. I took it as a **<<sign>>** that we should not go to the retreat that particular weekend. But *Xavier* insisted on going, and he kept looking among church members for someone who could do us the favor of taking us to the mountains.

By that time, we had already spent a whole year at the retreat, seeking for the **<<presence>>** of God through fasting and prayer every single weekend. In a certain sense, by now I was feeling somewhat tired because we had not experienced anything new within Mount Carmel. That specific day I wondered if I should continue with attending to the retreat or if I should stop altogether. Besides, I also thought about the many other things that I could be doing elsewhere, rather than spending so much time up there in the mountains. It was somewhere around nine o'clock in the evening on that same Friday when I was in my room, happy about the idea of getting a break from going to that place for a change. But to my surprise, *Xavier* arrived at my house at about 9:20 p.m., in a Chevrolet mini-van of a flashy green metallic color, and accompanied by a well-known member of the church. The brother's name is *Manuel,* he was at the wheel and he was willing to take us in his truck right at that hour. We all got into the car, and starting the journey, we reached the place sometime after eleven o'clock at night.

Unfortunately, Brother *Manuel* could not stay because he had to work the next day, on Saturday morning, so he returned to the city of Santa Ana as soon as he left us. Since we had no way to return home, Brother *Manuel* faithfully agreed to come back to pick us up on Sunday afternoon.

The morning arrived and we got up at seven o'clock to pray. Everything seemed normal but sometime later in the afternoon, a few uncommon things started to occur. My cousin *Theresa* started to faint during our stay in the retreat. My sister *Veronica* said that she felt as if some eyes were watching her the whole time, and that she felt under surveillance and uncomfortable. For my part, I was feeling terrible frustrated, and I considered that I was already wasting my time in that place. At about 2:00 in the afternoon a group of thirteen brothers came from another church and they gathered with us. The new brothers started praying for my cousin, and asking for divine healing inside one of the houses of the establishment. The pastors, *David* and *Priscilla,* were at the retreat but they were not with us in that particular praying reunion. Sister *Priscilla* had baptized the house where we were reunited with the name of *Lazarus.* In itself, the pastors had baptized each of the houses within the establishment with a name related to something biblical. The principal house or main house, was the pastoral house and it was baptized with the name of *House of David.* I will never forget that weekend because everything seemed to turn from bad to worse. Somewhere around nine-thirty p.m., on that extremely slow day, I was feeling quite **<<overwhelmed>>**. That Saturday night, with no moon in sight in the sky —*was especially dark.*

At that moment, even though I was in the same place where the group was praying, I was keeping a few steps away from them. I found myself silent, and with my face down, I looked only at the floor. I really did not want to be there anymore, and a very different kind of thoughts flooded my mind right then.

I began to wonder if it was perhaps because of me that there was not a divine manifestation. Inclusively, I even came to believe that perhaps my own disbelief and my inner hatred of humans had kept God away from us. Or possibly, the reason why God was not manifesting was that God did not love me because I was a bad person. And probably, since God hated me, he would not approach the prayer group meanwhile I was part of it. I also began to consider once more that God did not really exist and that everything I had experienced previously on the retreat, had been merely a series of unusual and inexplicable coincidences.

At this point, I kept telling myself:

—*If I had brought my car, I would be on my way home already.*

—*I no longer have anything to do here.*

However, when all those useless thoughts of a sore **<<looser>>** behaved like naughty little children – jumping up and down with total freedom inside my distressed intellect – the prayer group started screaming with joy, saying… *The Lord is here!*

At that same instant, some brothers burst into tears. Others began to speak in strange languages that I could not understand, and a couple more individuals were vibrating as if they were sick with the Parkinson's disease (*a neurological condition that makes a person to tremble uncontrollably*).

Surprised by the sudden change in attitude of the group, I preferred to keep my distance.

Notwithstanding, they continued in this manner for the space of a whole hour. After a while, it was almost midnight. Yet despite the fact that the group had been praying for several hours, they all looked fresh as a daisy. The brothers seemed to be full of joy and happiness. Just watching them, I was envious because I was feeling absolutely nothing more than just fatigue and disbelief, and all of this accompanied to the side by a great **<<apathy>>**.

Stubborn as a mule and entangled with my boring reflections, I continued to think that, indeed, it was now proven... God did not love me. But I thought that he had every reason no to love me since I really was not, nor had I ever been in my whole life, a man of good will.

And while all these fastidious ideas repeated themselves like a bell's echo inside me, suddenly, *Xavier* (*who had taken the position of leader of the prayer group*) said, raising his voice above everyone else:

—Who has not yet felt the presence of God?

I took the question as if it was exactly the opportunity I had been waiting for.

Therefrom, I immediately raised my right arm. At that moment, the whole group, as if they had all agreed in advance, took each other's hands and formed a big circle.

Next, they invited me to pass to the center of the loop. With my eyes still looking at the floor, I passed to the middle of the large wheel and instinctively closed my eyes without knowing what I could expect from all of this.

Right after that, the group began to pray with loud voices and with energy. Then, when barely fifteen minutes of prayer had passed, I heard a voice in a soft tone that whispered the following phrase into my right ear:

—Repent and confess your sins.

The voice sounded like that of a young man, but I could not identify it as belonging to a member of the group.

Out of mere curiosity, I immediately opened my eyes to see who had approached me to tell me such a thing, however, I did not see anyone that close to me.

Rather, when I opened my eyes, I realized that everyone in the group still had their eyes closed and were still firmly holding hands, forming the great circle around me.

I decided to closed my eyes again. Nevertheless, when the group had just spent approximately another five minutes into the prayer, the strange phenomenon happened for a second occasion…

Once more, I heard the same voice, but this time it was much closer to me. The person who talked was so proximate to my ear that it was as if the lips that pronounced the message were about to graze my right lobe (*lower part of the ear*). And the message was repeated:

– Repent and confess your sins.

But what was different was that on this occasion, the voice was not soft anymore, rather it spoke with a peculiar tone that gave it much seriousness and firmness. Yet again, I opened my eyes immediately to see who was saying such things. However, the situation repeated itself, there was no individual close enough to me to talk with such proximity.

I closed my eyes for the third time, still not knowing what to do or what to think about all this.

Nonetheless, what was happening to me was making me extremely nervous, as I already had the feeling that something out of the ordinary was taking place in my surroundings. But the phenomenon tripled, as soon as I closed my eyes the same voice appeared in my ear.

What was different was that now the voice sounded with a timbre of desperation.

And intoning a sound of distress and emergency, the mysterious voice screamed the same notice into my ear:

—I am telling you to confess all of your sins and to repent!

I could not contain myself any longer…

My legs weakened and I fell to my knees in the center of the circle. I felt that my heart had shattered as if it were a pot of clay that had just been violently thrown onto the floor. Then I broke whining like a little child, and I started to moan with loud crying and laments. There were so many tears in my eyes that I could not see well, for the same tears completely flooded my vision.

And although I was ashamed to say out loud my multitude of misdeeds in the presence of the people around me, I suffered that, and I endured my guilt. An atmosphere of urgency had been created in my heart, so I started to confess out loud each of my sins. One by one, I narrated my many deceptions, wicked ways, lies, thefts and other perversities I had committed since my childhood. I was telling God that I regretted every bad action. In addition, I told Jesus that I accepted him as the Lord and Savior of my life. I told Christ that I did not want to be the same man I had always been, that I surrendered to him, and that I was asking him to please forgive me and to accept me.

And from this unforgettable experience comes the third step to save your soul…

THIRD STEP TO SAVE THE SOUL

The third step is – **Repent**. This is about you repenting of your sins and accepting Jesus as your only Lord and Savior. Moreover, when you do it, do it with all of your heart, with all of your mind, and with all of your strength. Let us look at what the next scripture has to say concerning this:

> *Romans 10:9. So* ***YOU WILL BE SAVED****, if* ***YOU*** *honestly* ***SAY, "JESUS IS LORD,"*** *and if you believe* ***WITH ALL YOUR HEART*** *that God raised him from death.*

Since God cannot be deceived, for he knows the authentic intention of the heart, it is necessary for the person to show **<<real>>** repentance.

What this means is that if you truly repent, you will no longer commit the sins for which you have just repented. Repentance must be—*personal and legitimate* — for this to work. The Bible proves what I say, and this can be read in the book of Proverbs as follows:

> *Proverbs 28:13. Whoever hides their sins will not be successful, but* **WHOEVER CONFESSES** *their sins and stops doing wrong* ***WILL RECEIVE MERCY.***

It is necessary for you to know that if you accept Jesus as your Lord and Savior but you do not do it from your heart, you deceive yourself. And perhaps you can fool the person next to you, but you will never be able to fool God. That is why you honestly need to repent of your sins and make a true confession of your wrongdoings. Indeed, do this step with all your determination. And if you are one of those people who says that you do not have to do this because you are already righteous and good, please read what the following scripture states:

> *Romans 3:23.* ***ALL OF US HAVE SINNED*** *and fallen short of God's glory.*

Dear reader, do not fool yourself anymore. Acknowledge your necessity. Make a decision today and complete the third step **<<pronto>>**.

You do not have to pay anything to be saved. Nor are there expensive **<<rites>>** or elaborated ceremonies to reach God. This step is easy, and it is as close to you as in your own mouth and in your own heart. If you do not know how to start, you can follow this simple prayer:

—Lord Jesus Christ, I repent of my wickedness, please come into my life and fill the void in my heart with your presence. From today's date, I accept you as my Lord and as the only and sufficient Savior of my soul.

—From now on I am going to pray, fast, read the Bible, and congregate with brothers who really seek your presence in spirit and in truth.

—Father God, make your will be done to me. I do not want to live my life as I want, now I want to live my life as you want me to live it. Please guide me with your Holy Spirit. I also ask you to write my name in the Book of Life. Amen.

According to the Bible, the very specific way in which any human being can establish a connection with God, is not through science or some other secret method, but is right through Jesus. That is why, this was written:

> *John 14:6. Jesus answered, "I am the way, the truth, and the life.* **THE ONLY WAY TO THE FATHER IS THROUGH ME.**

CHAPTER 12

THE DAY THE WORLD ENDED

Why do most people insist on anticipating that the end of the world will be a collective event? There is a higher likelihood that death will come to a single person separately than that the destruction to all mankind will happen at the same time. I say this because for me – *the day of the end of the world* – came when I was only twenty years old. Being that this is the age when I died…

Now it was Sunday, in the wee hours of the morning. I was still at the retreat and I was still in the center of the circle that the prayer group had formed to pray for me. Also, I was still on my knees, crying. But the surprises had just begun… At a precise moment, the spiritual eyes of *Xavier* had been opened for just an instant and he had seen that something **<<abnormal>>** was happening in me. *Xavier* had seen that a head had just come out of my own head, and that this *new head* had a humanoid face… Although, it did not appear to be human at all (?).

Instead, the face resembled that of an animal or, to be more exact, of a giant insect (?). The truth is that *Xavier* immediately recognized that there was a malignant spirit inside me. Dear reader, I was **<<possessed>>** and I did not know it, for I have never accepted my spiritual experiences as real-life experiences. This, on the one hand, due to the fault of my exaggerated disbelief and on the other hand, due to my great ignorance of the spiritual realm. I think that what happened is that the entity that was inside me got nervous. The demon – *disturbed and frightened by the presence of God in that place* – had poked its head out of me as if trying to have a better look at what was going on outside of his hideout and shelter. *Xavier*, after recognizing that I was demon possessed, entered the great circle and put his hands on my head to rebuke the being from the underworld. As incredible as it may sound to the reader, at the very instant that *Xavier* settled his hand on the top of my head (*mid region*), a series of uncontrollable twitches overtook my body from head to toes. I started shaking and I could not control myself!

Without having a clue as to what was going on, I thought that something bad had already happened to my nervous system. I assumed that on this occasion, I had not been able to tolerate the **<<shock>>** of listening to the voices in my ear, and that I was finally having some sort of nervous breakdown.

In an attempt to regain composure, I slowly approached a wall on my knees to try to hold on to it and to try to control myself. But my efforts were useless. Grabbing myself from the wall did not help my situation. I tried to use reason, however, nothing was working. At that moment, my situation was somewhat precarious, ridiculous and intolerable. I continued crying like a baby, and now my whole body was convulsing without control. And, as if that were not enough, at this late hour of the night an electric storm began to fall on the surroundings of the mountain where we were located. It was not long when the outside of the house began to be pummeled by **<<deafening>>** thunder and lightning.

After just a few more minutes passed by, the thunderstorm was joined by a very strong rain and wind. The fierce wind of the tempest – *inexplicably angry* – was strongly hitting against the house, making it to tremble.

Something else that startled me at that moment, was that the windows of the house and the doors began to be beaten, and hard blows could be heard on the roof of the house (?).

It was as if violent people were out there lashing on all sides and corners the fragile pre-fabricated house made of only wood and cardboard. To add insult to injury, and to complete the scene, when all this was happening, I lifted my eyes only to see *Xavier* yelling into my face (!).

Xavier was yelling at me as if I were as distant as a block away. His strong cries rebuked me and with some dramatic words *Xavier* addressed me, saying:

—*Out of him! Demon, you have no part in the life of this man! He belongs to Jesus!*

I will never forget such scene. I was perplexed. Everything seemed crazy. Nothing made sense. Was I hallucinating? Was I dreaming? What was happening? Then, I simply wondered:

—*Is Xavier yelling at me?*

—*Why?*

I really did not understand anything, not in the least. It was as if I were living a scene from a horror movie, and the trouble was that I was the person who was getting the worst part. But the night was still young, and this was not over yet. It had only been the beginning, since it was going to get much worse for me...

The tension in the room was palpable. Some people remained steadfast, praying with their eyes closed. However, there were others who seemed terrified and were merely looking around, and I believe that they did not know whether to stay or rather, to rush out of the place. Some people around me looked extremely nervous. I saw that a few of them had a cold sweat, because I could see drops of sweat running down the forehead, and temples of one or another individual.

By then, I was still kneeling, crying, and shaking. I had not had even a minimum of success in trying to stand up over and over again.

In the meantime, in the midst of massive electrical discharges, the storm continued relentlessly, illuminating the large windows of the mobile home with numerous and spectacular lightning strikes. The resounding sound of every clap of thunder was making the earth tremble, letting us know that the storm was right above us. By that time, it was already about two o'clock a.m., on Sunday morning but the surprises were not over yet.

All of a sudden, and in what appeared to be a completely irrational act to me, without minding the tempest outside the house, *Xavier* proceeded to open the main entrance door of the house, leaving it wide open.

Right after that, in a grave tone and with a commanding voice, *Xavier,* who continued shouting into my face, expressed himself in the following manner:

—Demon! Jesus has told me that you are cast out at this precise second!

At that point, solemn and vibrant, *Xavier* added a prolonged word... **NOW!**

And when he shouted this word to me, I felt that a powerful gust of wind rose from my chest, to then come out impetuously throughout the principal door of the house that *Xavier* himself had opened.

As soon as that gust of wind came out of me and left the house, *Xavier*, perfectly aware of what had just happened, immediately closed the door, slamming it shut with a single pull.

Apparently, the demon that had been inside me was finally gone. When that – *infernal entity* – left my body, I felt that my heart had literally being ripped out of my chest. The pain was brutal and I quickly lifted up my t-shirt, as I thought I was going to see a hole in my chest. When I examined my body, everything looked normal, at least on the surface of my skin. Then I had the idea that my heart had exploded because of the many astonishments I had experienced, and I thought that I was living my last seconds of life on Earth. I confess that believing that my heart had exploded was an absurd assumption on my part. However, regarding the fact that I had little time left to live, I was not so wrong because what I was about to experience next would surprise me once again. The incredible pain in my chest would not stop, and because of that I was writhing in pain on the floor. The pain was so excruciating and unbearable that I wanted to leave the house quickly and ask for help, and to call an ambulance in those small hours of the morning. So, as I could, I finally got to my feet. And wobbling like a dizzy drunkard after a night of partying, I rushed towards the door to escape from there when, suddenly, I received a sharp **<<blow>>** to the chest...

The impact was so strong and so abrupt that I fell onto the ground like a freshly cut tree, and I fell on my back, face up. And there, lying on the floor, I turned my head to all sides, and with my eyes open very wide, I looked around to see who had hit me.

My initial fright turned into **<<terror>>** when I realized that no human being had touched me– *and I knew it*– since I had not seen anyone hitting me.

Lying on the floor, I made a new attempt to stand up to run out of the house, and to call for help – *but something* – prevented me from doing so.

At that moment, *Xavier's* spiritual eyes were opened again, and with better clarity he was able to see the demon that was harassing me. *Xavier* said that the creature was like an oversized arachnid. He told me that this demonic being surpassed me in stature and that my 5.7 feet in height was dwarfed in front of the creature. The being had an **<<armor>>** that looked extremely hard and it had glossy black polished color. The beast also had a tail and a stinger, as well as six legs that each ended with crusher claws. With its hind legs it stood vertically and reached the inner roof of the house, which measured a little bit over 7.9 feet in height. From that information, I now know that the demon of hatred is shaped like a scorpion or like some other type of an unknown arachnid.

In the same way, I also know that this repugnant being embraces the heart of man by using its numerous members and pincers. And with the sting of its tail, it infects the human heart with the poison of revenge and hatred. The demon of hate has an armored shell that is specially **<<hardened>>** and it is reinforced like that in order to never let love pass through it.

The same malignant spirit that had been cast out of me just a few minutes before, had now returned to perpetrate its cruel revenge. I was not seeing anyone attacking me. Nevertheless, when I tried to stand up, I could not because, by utilizing its multiple extremities, that demonic creature had taken hold of my hands and of my feet. My fear increased twofold because I had been left completely helpless and paralyzed.

After immobilizing me, the demon started to hit me on the chest. The huge – *infernal scorpion* – was crashing its heavy carapace against me, and he was doing it over and over again with great fury to get into my body, to take possession of me once more. His blows were so strong that I felt as though my life was escaping from my body, just as smoke slips away between the fingers. And during one of those many impacts, I finally ended up losing my consciousness.

However, that had not finished my suffering. The nightmare had just started…

ROADWAY TO HELL

When I opened my eyes, I was no longer inside the house of *Lazarus*. Nor I was next to the prayer group anymore. In the same manner, I no longer had any demon beating me on the chest – *to my good fortune*. But to my bad luck and to continue with the surprises, I also was not lying on the floor on my back, facing up and looking at the ceiling inside the house. Instead, I was now upside down and squarely facing the entrance of what appeared to be – an obscure and macabre abysmal pit. It was a sinister tunnel whose bottom I could not see. The hole was formed by a **<<funereal>>** darkness that seemed to absorb all light. The mouth of the deep pit had a circumference of about one hundred feet in diameter, and I found myself alone and flying over its entrance, just as though I was levitating above it. I struggled to reassure myself. Now more than ever I had to use logic. I tried once and again to rationalize what had happened, but it was impossible–I had been dominated by panic and confusion. It took me some time to know what was happening, and I could not believe it, as was my habit. At that moment, I had the following thoughts…

—But just a moment ago, I was crying inside a house…

—What happened?

—Where am I now?

—Could it be that…?

—No, no it can't be…!

—Did I die?

And sadly, the cruel reality was beginning to take shape. A change that I notice in me was that my body was no longer trembling frantically. Nor I was crying more. My face, my eyes, and my t-shirt were **<<dry>>** of tears. In a similar manner, I notice that I was completely aware of all my senses. I could think, breath, feel, see, and hear. It is interesting to note that once the human spirit leaves its physical body, it is difficult to distinguish the boundary between what is the material body, and what is the spiritual body. In itself, the difference is — *actually minimal.*

In the biblical passage in the second letter to the Corinthians in chapter twelve, the Apostle Paul gives an account of a separation between — *the physical body and the spiritual body* — that he himself experienced. And he tells us that when he was taken to the third heaven, he himself was not able to discern at that moment whether he had been taken to that other dimension in his spiritual body or in his material body. Therefore, I had all of my faculties and all of my cognitive, sensory, and locomotive capabilities (*intellectual ability, perceptive, and mobility of the body*).

Notwithstanding, one thing I could not do was run away from there because I was sustained as if levitating in the air. Despite all the struggling and kicking I did, I could not move a single inch from the center of the immense black abysmal pit which seemed to head directly towards the very own center of the Earth. I felt helpless and useless. And now, who could I turn to for help?

In the **<<shadow>>** of the remembrances of my mind, I thought that I could have been a better person – *a better son, brother, and friend*. The memories of my past life were tormenting me. But now what could I do? I was where I was, things were as they were, and not as I wanted them to be. I began to resign myself to my tragedy. I felt helpless and defeated. I understood that although in life I had always believed myself a self-sufficient person, I was nothing but a weakling human, without strength and without any special powers. And what was even worse than that is that now – *I did not even have hope to better myself or to change anything at all.*

It took me a bit of time to become fully aware of where I was, for I thought that it was all a dream, or better said, a whole nightmare. Nevertheless, this horrible *excessive daydreaming (maladaptive daydream*) was not over yet, as I slowly started to sink into the pit.

Little by little, my body was descending towards the bottom of the silent, somber, and very tenebrous tunnel…

All at once, distant, barely perceptible under the silence and bathed in an absolute **<<darkness>>** I began to hear noises. Restlessly, I paid more attention and stopped moving. My already existing anguish turned into a deranged terror, because…

Coming from the bottom of the tunnel, I started to hear the screams of many people! There seemed to be thousands of people down there at the bottom of the pit. The voices indicated as much. The howlings were so horrifying that it sounded as though the people who were screaming were being cut in half with a rustic hand saw made to cut wood. The lower I descended, the more the laments increased. The screams grew louder and louder. I started moving with abrupt and frantic movements of my hands and feet. I wanted to scape my destiny. I wanted to run away from there. I wished to wake up from that nightmare. I pinched myself, I scratched myself, I bit my hands and my forearms, but everything I did was useless. Nothing could awaken me from this horrible reality. I kept descending inside the tunnel of the great pit for what seemed to be – a whole eternity. And I remained inside the hole long enough to understand that none of this – *was a lucid dream or a fruit of a vivid imagination*. Also, to make me realize that as sad and as incredible as it seemed to me, I was no longer in the world of the living.

But I still had not reached the bottom of this underground passage. Instead, I remained hanging in **<<suspense>>** and descending with great slowness.

But then again, why were there human cries in that place? What sort of tragedy was going on down there? Those were valid questions. However, I did not want to learn those answers in person.

After some time had passed and I had calmed a little, I remembered that I had accepted Jesus when I was still alive on Earth. And having accomplished this leap of faith moments ago, when I was still inside the house of *Lazarus*, lit a spark of hope inside me. Because I knew that this time I had <<indeed>> accepted Christ with all of my heart, and with a true repentance.

And while I was still flying over the mouth of hell and without even knowing if anyone would even listen to me, I started to scream, to shout and to say:

—I do not belong to this place!

—I belong to Jesus!

—When I was in the World, I repented!

Although, there was no immediate response. Even so, I repeated the same cries for a long time.

In the meantime, the howling I heard coming from the bottom of the tunnel continued to send chills all along my spine, and to make my hair stand on end.

CHAPTER 13

A NEW PLACE

I was still inside the tunnel to hell, when I was hastily transposed into a different world, immediately finding myself somewhere else. In the spiritual body, traveling from one place to another one happens extremely quickly. It is as fleeting as the blink of an eye because the spiritual body is not subject to the physical laws that we commonly know.

Now I was in an infinitely better place, for I was among the clouds and I was free. I could move and walk. Thus, I started to jump for joy! My memory, momentarily **<<eclipsed>>** by the swift transposition of dimensions, regained its consciousness anew and made me aware of my new state of life. And somehow, I realized that the former nature I knew of time and space, no longer prevailed. Now I was in the zone of – *no time* – *and in heaven*. But one may ask, what does heaven look like? I will describe it right away…

I did not see heaven colored in any other hue but its usual color, and intense celestial blue. The clouds also did not show a different range than their normal tone, a white that shined with the reflection of the light. What was different is that now I could walk on the clouds. At first, the spiritual realm seemed to be identical to the material world. But somehow, I knew and realized that I was no longer in the earthly physical world that I used to live in. It was exceptionally beautiful to be in that place. The **<<tranquility>>** and the peace soaked into every corner of the atmosphere. I was fascinated but I restrained myself a bit. After sometime, I gain confidence, I got curious, therefore I started to walk on the clouds. I took a deep breath and drank in the moisture and freshness of the clouds around me. The brief walk provided me with a spectacular view of the new earth that could be seen under the sky. I looked for the sun, however, I could not find it. Nevertheless, everything was very well lit, as if under the full light of a warm and sunny afternoon. Something that equally amazed me was that in heaven the air is neither cold nor hot because the air adjusts itself to the body temperature of each individual person. What that means, is that the air is a perfect fit for each individual. I also noticed that the same air seemed to caress my face, as I felt as if delicate hands were passing along my face when the wind blew towards me.

In the meantime, I was still walking on the clouds and looking around with astonishment saying to myself:

—*Wow!*

—*I died!*

—*How nice!*

And there I was, when just right in front of me and about three hundred feet away, I started to distinguish the silhouette of what seemed to be a human being. I stopped to pay a close attention. The apparition was walking towards me at a moderate pace. When the figure came closer, I could tell that it was a character of a considerable height, dressed in a long robe and easily making his way through the clouds.

How great was my bewilderment to see who it was…!

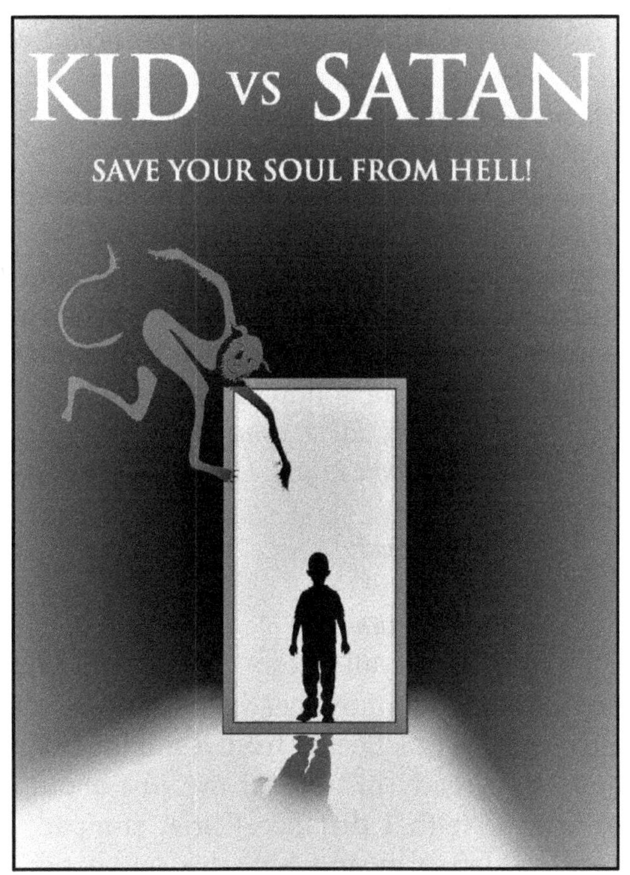
KID VS SATAN
SAVE YOUR SOUL FROM HELL!

It was Jesus!

But if the reader believes that I experienced delight upon seeing him, my dear reader is greatly mistaken, because I immediately thought:

—*Oh, no!*

—*I have been brought here only to be judged!*

—*He is going to condemn me for all my misdeeds on Earth!*

—*I will be sent back to the pit of Hell!*

And my feelings of jubilation at being in heaven did not last long because all of my happiness turned into fear. Afraid, I began to tremble. The more Jesus Christ approached me, the more I trembled with panic. At that moment, I had in my mind the following phrases:

—*Please stop, do not come to me!*

—*I cannot come to you, I have too many things to fix in my life!*

—*I am not ready!*

—*Have mercy!*

—*Is not my time yet!*

And when all these stormy reflections were jumping out of my head almost at the same time — just as rats fleeing from a sinking boat — Jesus was already in front of me, just about six feet away. At that distance Christ stopped, he raised his left arm and with his left hand, he pointed his index finger towards me. I felt as though I were going to pass out. I only expected the worst. Eternal damnation was guaranteed and taken for granted.

The day of my judgment had come, and now I was just waiting for the verdict and the sentence. My heart was in my throat. I gritted my teeth. I could not breathe. I opened my eyes as wide as I could.

And with a knot in my stomach, I said to myself:

—*Enjoy these last few seconds in heaven, for they will be your last.*

—*Surely, I will be dropped to hell as fast as a lightning, just as it happened with Satan* (*see Luke 10:18*).

All of these different of propositions and approaches were circulating within me, when after a dense silence, Jesus Christ pronounced the following words...

– You are one more of my people…

His <<seven>> words uttered in a sincere tone and without reproach, caused me the greatest joy of my existence. I felt I regained my life at that instant and the relief helped me to breathe again.

After that, he held out his arms. I accepted his invitation and joyfully walked towards him. I rested my head in Jesus and leaning against his chest, I felt like a baby. I felt that I had just been born and that I was in the arms of my progenitor. And I could feel the good will and the infinite tenderness that can emanate only from a being full of *compassion*. And there… Listening to his heartbeat, I could feel the **<<love>>** of Jesus Christ. His love… As an invisible force that I could not see but only feel – *it is like an energy* – and this energy was so great that it filled every single part of my being. And when my body could not contain such a great energy, I felt that this love was going through every pore of my being as if it were radiation.

I could literally feel that this love had such grandiose power, that while passing through me as in the form of radiation, it extended and dissipated itself towards the infinite Universe that was behind me.

Oh, that love so full of power! So admirable, wonderful, incomparable, and majestic. Like that without limits, is the love of God.

It seems to me that I experienced the same thing the Apostle Paul did when he was taken to heaven nearly two thousand years ago. I am still referring to the experience that Saint Paul himself talks about in the second letter to the Corinthians, in chapter twelve.

Brother Paul in the same way speaks about this **<<powerful>>** love of God, and also attempts to describe it by sharing with us the next words:

> *Romans 8:38-39. Yes,* ***I AM SURE*** *that* ***NOTHING CAN SEPARATE US FROM GOD'S LOVE****—not death, life, angels, or ruling spirits. I am sure that nothing now, nothing in the future, no powers, nothing above us or nothing below us—nothing in the whole created world—will ever be able to separate us from the love God has shown us in Christ Jesus our Lord.*

Dear relatives, brothers in faith, friends and readers... Is God not beautiful and generous? Look at how much does God loves us!

Then again, speaking of the beauty of God, maybe someone will ask, what is Jesus like?

Very well, I will describe him next...

Jesus Christ is tall, about 6.3 feet in height. His skin is white. I also noted that his body is of a medium build.

His hair is the color of twenty-four-karat gold. If you have gold in front of you, ask if it is a 24-karat gold. If it is so, then you are seeing the color of the hair of Jesus — *the redeemer of the souls.* He parts his hair in the middle. His hair is straight and long, and the long of his hair makes a small curvature as it reaches his shoulders and back.

His majesty at that moment was simple but stunning because he did not wear jewelry, or rings, or crowns. He did not held titles, or swords, or shields. He did not even have an escort. He walked alone, covered with a simple and plain mantle, and not even his robe had decorations or the sophisticated embroidery worn by any royalty. His smooth, white tunic looked as though it had no seems, belts, emblems, or symbols. His mantle was long, but it did not cover his hands and feet.

Jesus happily walked barefoot through the clouds.

I touched his hands and when I leaned on his chest, I was fascinated when I watched his face. Notwithstanding, I cannot remember his face — I do not know why — and that is the reason why I cannot describe it in this short compilation of memories.

It is important to add that if on Earth you have to watch your thoughts – *you must also do so in Heaven.* I made a thinking mistake while in heaven, and an invisible being did not even take more than a second to correct me. And since I do not want to make of this issue a <<mystery>> I will tell what happened...

When I was laying on the chest of Jesus, and fascinated I was watching his face, I was thinking:

–I do not like this man. More likely...

–I love this man!

But a **<<residue>>** within the subconscious of my former human nature betrayed me. Suddenly my mind had doubts. Because of that, I did reconsider my last thought. So, I thought for a second time trying to correct:

–Wait a minute... If I am in love with this man... Am I a homosexual?

At that point, I immediately had this other thought:

–Oh no, my God! Please do not add that I am attracted to men to the long list of things I already have to fix in me!

And it had only been about a fraction of a second after my last thought, when some invisible being corrected me. An audible voice pronounced in my right ear, with a little cry of reproach:

–No!

–This love is pure, without spot or wrinkle!

Afterwards, already with the permission of that invisible voice, marveled, I **<<adored>>** Jesus Christ not only with my eyes but now also with all of my heart.

At that moment, I could not see who had said such a thing. However, months later and during another experience I had, I learned that the Holy Spirit has the power to speak and to reproof humans. And he can do it – even with an audible voice – if he believes that it is convenient to do so.

Unfortunately, I did not stay in heaven with Jesus. Just as I had suddenly reached heaven, I was transposed back to my physical body in an opening and closing of the eyes.

My body of glory and victory over death, became once more a body of tears, sobbing, and lament. And on a new account, I was inside the house of *Lazarus* with *Veronica, Theresa, Xavier* and my other brothers in faith.

When I opened my eyes, I was still lying on the floor, facing up and looking towards the ceiling, which bore an insipid light cream color.

But at least the gigantic infernal scorpion that was harassing and battering me, was already gone.

Finally, I could stand on my feet without getting beat up anymore. Nevertheless, as soon as I found myself standing up, *Xavier* ordered me to read the Bible.

I refused flatly.

Because, besides the fact that I was not experiencing the slightest desire to read, I did not feel in any way **<<capable>>** of reading absolutely anything.

I was still weeping buckets, and my whole body continued shaking from my head to my toes.

I still could not make it clear what was going on and my physical ruin was total. And I kept on crying and shaking for three consecutive days. The pain on my heart was so great that the ailment in my chest lasted three long months (I provide this information so that reader can imagine the precarious situation I was going through at that time).

By then it was around three-thirty in the morning on the same Sunday, and although I had just had a divine revelation of Jesus Christ, Heaven, and of the tunnel that leads to Hell – *I was not resting in a bed of roses*. Everything was confusing, painful, anguishing, and full of suffering for me.

Regardless, *Xavier* strongly insisted that I had to read (because he was being commanded by the Holy Spirit). Therefore, he held my hands and placed the Bible on both of my palms. Then, *Xavier* said urgently:

– You have to read!

– You will not be completely set free if you do not read now!

– You really have to do it!

It was super hard for me to simply hold the sacred book, because both of my hands were shaking madly.

I felt that my eyes were swollen from crying and my vision was still full of tears, and if I could barely see the figure of *Xavier* in front of me... How did *Xavier* want me to read the miniscule letters of the biblical book?

But I tried. And when I opened the Bible, the pages of the book passed along by themselves from one place to another, finally stopping at the book of Psalms, chapters fifty-five to fifty-seven. These Psalms stood out above the rest of the scriptures as if illuminated by a dim light, and I focused my efforts on trying to read these scriptures in particular.

My amazement was that when I began to read these manuscripts, I felt that they gave me a <<special>> strength within me. These ancient writings that were thousands of years old, as incredible as it may seem – *narrated my experience of life and death* – that I had just passed through a few minutes earlier. At least that is how I understood this, since the scripture related **<<specifically>>** mi suffering and my anguish on that night. The Bible consoled me, and I felt that God himself was speaking to me through this sacred scripture. In the following pages I write part of these Psalms, and I emphasize the words and verses that I understood were speaking of my particular situation.

Psalm 55:

1-GOD, HEAR MY PRAYER. DON'T
IGNORE MY CRY FOR HELP.
2-Please listen and answer me. Let me speak to you and tell you what upsets me.
*3-**MY ENEMIES** shout at me and **THREATEN ME. IN THEIR ANGER THEY ATTACK ME. THEY BRING TROUBLES CRASHING DOWN ON ME.***
4-MY HEART IS POUNDING INSIDE ME. I AM AFRAID TO DIE.
5-I AM TREMBLING WITH FEAR. I AM TERRIFIED!
*6-Oh, **I WISH** I had wings like a dove. **I WOULD FLY AWAY** and find a place to rest.*
7- I would go far into the desert and stay there.
8-I WOULD RUN AWAY.
*9-**MY LORD**, confuse their words and **STOP THEIR PLANS**. I see much cruelty and fighting in this city.*
*16-**I WILL CALL TO GOD FOR HELP**, and the Lord will save me.*
*17-I speak to God morning, noon, and night. I tell him what upsets me, and **HE LISTENS TO ME!***
18-I have fought in many battles, but he has always rescued me and brought me back safely.

Psalm 56:
*1-**God, people have attacked me**, so be*
merciful to me. They have been chasing me all
day, closing in to attack me.
*2-**My enemies come at me constantly**. There*
are too many fighters to count.
*3-**When I am afraid, I put my trust in you.***
4-I trust God, so I am not afraid of what people
can do to me!
*5-**My enemies are always making plans***
against me.
6-They hide together and watch every move I
make, hoping for some way to kill me.
7-God, send them away because of the bad things
they did. Show your anger and defeat those
people.
*8-**You know I am very upset. You know how***
much I have cried. Surely you have kept and
account of all my tears.
9-I know that when I call for help, my enemies
will turn and run. I know that because God is
with me!
10-I praise God for his promise to me.
11-I trust God, so I am not afraid of what people
can do to me!
12-God, I will keep the special promises I made to
you. I will give you my thank offering.
*13-**YOU SAVED ME FROM DEATH**. You*
kept me from being defeated. So, I will serve you
in the light that only the living can see.

Psalms 57:
*1-**GOD**, be merciful to me. Be kind because my soul trusts in you. **I HAVE COME TO YOU FOR PROTECTION**,* while the trouble passes.
2-**I PRAY TO GOD MOST HIGH FOR HELP**, and he takes care of me completely!
3-**FROM HEAVEN** he helps me and saves me. **GOD WILL** remain loyal to me and **SEND HIS LOVE TO PROTECT ME.**
4-**MY LIFE IS IN DANGER**. My enemies are all around me. They are like man-eating lions,
6-**MY ENEMIES SET A TRAP FOR MY FEET TO BRING ME DOWN. THEY DUG A DEEP PIT TO CATCH ME,**

I read those Psalms again and again, and this written word gave me inner peace. At last the storm stopped. The rain and the lightning ceased, and after 2 more hours the day began to shine and shimmer. I saw the first rays of the sun seep through the windows of the house, and I felt more confident with the dawn of the new day. As at about 5 a.m., I stopped the repetitive reading, and exhausted, fell asleep. After an hour and a half, I woke up, but my body did not stop shaking, nor could I stop crying. Frightened to the depths of my soul by what had happened to me that night, I went out to look for the pastors to ask for help.

CHAPTER 14

THE FIRE FROM HEAVEN

It was Sunday and very early in the morning when I knocked on the door of the pastors. They were people who rose early to pray, and by then they were wide awake.

Brother *David* and Sister *Priscilla* paid immediate attention to me. Crying and sobbing, I told them about what had just happened to me, and they understood me – *I think*. I asked them to pray for me because I felt as though I was experiencing a very critic health condition. It was so bad that I thought I was going to die again. I asked the pastors:

–*Why can't I stop crying?*

–*Why can't my body stop shaking?*

–*What it is happening to me?*

They did not have immediate answers for me. Nevertheless, they agreed to pray for me, and we went to pray inside the miniature-church in the main house of the retreat.

After being in prayer for about half an hour, the brothers who had been praying with us on Saturday and in the early hours of Sunday began to arrive. It did not take long before *Veronica, Theresa, and Xavier* also arrived and a large group of prayer was formed again. It would not be an hour in group prayer before something wonderful happened again because... The Holy Spirit fell in the place! And the madness started all over again!

Then the situation became chaotic. Some brothers fell onto the ground like planks, as if they had fainted. Some cried. Others were trembling. Four more people spoke a language I could not understand. Moreover, I saw *Xavier* jumping and saying repeatedly:

—I am burning, I am burning!

And *Xavier* jumped and twisted around as if wanting to shake something that no one else could see. On my part, I found myself kneeling on the floor, feeling as though a powerful electric current had taken over me. That electricity, which seemed to be thousands of volts, came and went – *like a wave of the sea* – running from my head to my toes in a constant sway. It was an amazing power, but far from feeling comfortable, I felt as if I were going to explode and that I would die again. This time the craziness had been collective. Every one experienced something different at that moment. And this time who could I turn to ask for help if we all were in the same situation?

At that, I heard the sound of an ambulance's <<sirens>> in the distance, but I thought that the alarm noise was all part of the dementia that we were all experiencing. What surprise I felt when... A fire truck arrived at Mount Carmel!

What had happened was that the neighbors from the surrounding areas had seen that the roof of the house where we were praying was engulfed in flames. The neighbors, thinking that the house was burning, called the fire department.

Consequently, the firefighters arrived and searched for literal fire to quench – *but the fire was spiritual in nature*. The firemen, finding no physical fire, and not being able to understand what was happening in that place, left immediately. When the manifestation of the Holy Spirit ended, everyone in the retreat did not cease to speak of what we had all experienced, and so we spent the rest of the day talking about the wonders of God.

Later in the evening, Brother *Manuel* came back for us and we returned to the city of Santa Ana on that same Sunday night. Once at home, I stayed locked in my room until Tuesday because I was spending that time crying and trembling.

We had encounter so many supernatural experiences at Mount Carmel in just one weekend that I was **<<astonished>>** and was still not able to recover.

When I finally felt better, I started attending church every day of service, and I attended in the company of *Veronica, Theresa and Xavier*. And from this extraordinary experience comes the fourth step to knowing God, and saving your soul…

Real-Life History
KID
VS
SATAN
save your soul from hell!
VIRGO ZUSA

FOURTH STEP TO SAVE THE SOUL

The fourth step and last step to save your soul is – **Seek for the baptism in the Holy Spirit**. If you have accepted Jesus Christ with all your heart and then immediately you die after having performed that act of faith – *you go to heaven*. However, if God gives you permission to live one more day after accepting Jesus as your only Lord and Savior… Seek for the baptism in the Holy Spirit with all your strength! Seek for its plenitude and fullness!

Just as you desire water when you are thirsty. Just as you look for survival itself… Seek for it. Do not let yourself live in spiritual poverty. Now, about the baptism in the Holy Spirit, the Bible states the following:

Luke 3:16. John said, "I am just baptizing with water. But someone more powerful is going to come, and I am not good enough even to untie his sandals. ***HE*** *will* ***BAPTIZE YOU*** *with the* ***HOLY SPIRIT*** *and with fire.*

That scripture is about John the Baptist prophesying that Jesus is the one who baptizes with the Holy Spirit. The following verse tell us about the wonder of the spiritual union with God.

Romans 8:16. And the ***SPIRIT*** *himself speaks to our* ***spirits*** *and* ***MAKE US SURE*** *that we are God's children.*

In this paragraph, the word <<spirit>> written with a capital letter means the Spirit of God, and the word spirit with a lowercase letter symbolizes the spirit of man. Therefore, the **Spirit** of God is united with the **spirit** of a human being in the baptism with the Holy Spirit.

For this reason – *this is not a maybe or a perhaps* – the individual who has been baptized by the Holy Spirit, knows, discerns and is **100%** certain that he is a <<legitimate>> citizen of the Celestial Kingdom because he knows it and he can feel it so. And probably someone may wonder, how can I in the same way receive the baptism in the Holy Spirit?

Well, we (*Veronica, Theresa, Xavier and I*) received it through prayer, fasting, and by the laying of the hands. The Bible also gives us information as to how to obtain it. Let us look:

> *Acts 8:15. When Peter and John arrived,* ***THEY PRAYED*** *for the Samaritan believers* ***TO RECEIVE*** *the Holy Spirit.*

> *Acts 8:17. Peter and John then* ***PLACED THEIR HANDS*** *on everyone who had faith in the Lord, and they* ***WERE GIVEN*** *the Holy Spirit.*

Here we can see that the baptism in the Holy Spirit is sought in prayer, and also by the laying of hands of the brothers in Christ who **<<already>>** have the Holy Spirit within them. Nevertheless, in other instances the baptism in the Holy Spirit can also fall on people who are listening to preaching discourses by those brothers who likewise <<already>> have the Holy Spirit inside them. This can be read in the book of Acts, chapter ten with verse forty-four, and in chapter eleven, with line fifteen. In other words – *God's people give because they have.* If you have never heard anything like this, you are not alone, as religion has overseen hiding this fact very well.

CHAPTER 15
FINAL NOTES

Dear reader, this is a history with a happy ending. My cousin had been healed that same weekend at the retreat. However, for three consecutive days *Theresa* could not speak Spanish because she was one of the people who learned to speak in strange tongues during the baptism in the Holy Spirit. Also, another strange thing she experienced is that she could not write in Spanish for several days. Instead, she wrote entire pages of strange symbols whose meaning we could never decipher. Anyhow, *Theresa* looked happy and radiant, and since that day up to our present day, she has been free of her fainting spells and the other problems she had experienced that were spiritual in nature.

Theresa and Xavier later married and now they live happily with their two children in Riverside, California. My sister Veronica also married, and she lives equally happy with her husband and children in San Diego, California.

I still have not married, and thus far I have dedicated myself to being a regular member of a church and living in San Diego, California. For now, I have plans to spread the good news of salvation, and I hope to do so, in part, with the help of this book. By the way, my mantra during this current period of my life is:

—*God lives!*

EXORCISM AND MIRACLE HEALING

Here in this section, I write about some things that I have learned during my life as a Christian. I hope that these brief annotations that I have assimilated from my Christian life and from the Bible may be useful in your own life as a faithful follower of Jesus.

I was fifteen years old when a demon struck and hurt my stomach. What I have not narrated is that my martyrdom of having that wound on my body lasted seven long years. So, it was a long time of constant lamentation, stabbing pain, and cramps in my intestines.

But one day when I was twenty-two years old, Jesus healed me miraculously. By that time, two years had already passed since everything we had experienced at the Mount Carmel retreat. And this is what happened…

Seeking miraculous healing for the problem I had in my stomach, one day I attended a campaign of – *divine healing* – that was being held at a church named Calvary Temple located in Santa Ana, California. The campaign lasted three days, and even though many people testified about having healed during the campaign, I myself did not heal. Nevertheless, when the campaign ended, before saying goodbye the preacher gave one last advice to the congregation gathered there, saying:

–If you did not heal during this campaign, do not worry, declare your healing as done.

–Own your healing.

–This is going to be your medicine… From now on, even if you feel the disease that afflicts you, declare that you are healthy and insist that you are healthy until your health comes.

By the way, the preacher of that campaign was the brother evangelist *Roy of the Garza*. I took the advice with good grace, and after declaring my healing daily for about two months straight, I testify in writing that Jesus the messiah had miraculously healed me.

Right now, I will narrate how that came to be…

After proclaiming my healing, as I did every evening, one night I slept. While asleep, I saw that Jesus had entered my room, and I could only think at that moment:

—God's healing has arrived!

As soon as Christ came into my room, he leaned over to my side and inserted his two hands into my stomach, moving my intestines. In this way, he **<<repaired>>** the damage that the demon had caused. My physical body could not awaken because I had fallen into a deep sleep, but with my spiritual eyes I was able to see what happened. I managed to see and feel his hands entering my stomach, and I could feel how he moved my intestines from side to side. The good thing is that I felt no pain during this divine surgery, and from that day until today I have been healthy, to God's glory, of course. It seems to me that I now understand what happened to Adam in the biblical story in the book of Genesis, chapter two, with verse twenty-one, when God took one of Adam's ribs to create the woman (*Eve*). Adam saw all that had happened, but he could not awaken, for in him a *deep sleep* had fallen. However, his spiritual body was awake, and for that reason he knew everything that had happened because Adam had not yet sinned and still had full spiritual communion with God. Yet, I dare to say that you have to be careful with all the miraculous healings. But... Why do I say so, the reader may ask?

I say such thing because the person who has been miraculously healed or who has been freed from the possession of evil spirits will be put to the test. Because after I was healed by God, I was immediately attacked by the fiery darts of Satan called **<<doubt>>**. What happened to me was that very often I was giving a fairly strong pang in the navel. Notwithstanding, I resisted my symptoms by saying to myself:

—I am not sick for Jesus healed me!

Doing this kept me healthy because I did not accept sickness back into my body. It is important to talk about this because the devil always wants to sow doubt in the human heart. When someone heals miraculously, the evil cherubim Lucifer returns to give a sting or a thump to that person, just as if the original ailment had returned, but it is all a lie. Satan does this to test – *whether the individual really believes* – in God's healing or in His divine deliverance.

Doubt is like a two-edged sword in the hands of Satan, and he uses this weapon very skillfully in the following manner... To start, he strikes the person with the first edge of the sword. This initial attack is an invitation of sorts to doubt. If the person relents and believes that the symptoms of the disease have returned, it is almost certain that the disease will be <<put>> back in the individual. However, this is not done by God, but by the Devil himself.

After that, to complete his attack and with all the rage of the world, the demon turns the sword and gives a second blow. At that point, the condition returns but now the person's later state may be more awful than his illness state was at the beginning. I mention this because of what is written in the book of Matthew chapter twelve, with verses forty-three, to forty-five. Since, according to this teaching, the ultimate condition of the individual can worsen by up to seven times.

The *trick* to staying healthy or free after a divine intervention by God is to not give the devil any opportunity. The Christian must be a – *firm believer* – in that what God has done, he has done it well. When God miraculously heals someone, or when he releases someone from the yoke of demons, no matter what kind of bond this has been... Watch out for the fiery darts of Satan!

This is because the Prince of Darkness is not going to stand there, crossing his arms and watching how the person enjoys the miracle that God has performed in his life. Therefore, it is necessary to do as it is wisely put in writing in the book of James:

> *James 4:7. So give yourselves to God.* ***STAND AGAINST*** *the devil, and* ***HE WILL RUN AWAY*** *from you.*

Moreover, besides resisting the doubt that Satan wants to **<<forcefully>>** impose on the person, it is advisable for the believer to – *cover himself with God's armor* – on a daily basis. All this information about the spiritual armor can be found in Saint Paul's letter to the Ephesians chapter six, with verses from ten to eighteen. In the same way, I advise the new believer to remain in communion with the brothers in faith, visiting the church every day of service. That way you will keep the victory that God has already given you.

GOD KNOWS YOUR FUTURE

One of the many titles God has is <<omniscient>>. This word means that he knows everything. With that in mind, if God knows everything, then he knows the past, the present, and what will happen in the future. As the reader can tell from what has been read in a past chapter of this book, God knew that I would die, and that I would go to hell if I did not repent of all my evils. For that reason – the Holy Spirit insisted even with shouts in my ear – because Jesus knows that our destiny in disobedience to the Heavenly Father is only death.

The Bible is <<packed>> from beginning to end with stories about how God's knowledge of the future – *alerted people* – to help them to preserve their lives. However, it is important to make it known that God can only warn us. He will not make the decision for us. This is because God wants to respect our– *sovereign will*. For he has already given us the **<<power>>** to make our own judgments and to make our own decisions.

WHY FASTING?

Every time we went to the retreat, we went in complete fasting and prayer. We did not drink any water, nor did we eat anything, while we stayed inside the place. Fasting is very important because it make us **<<one>>** with God. As the months passed, I learned that fasting serves the purpose of uniting – *our physical body with our spiritual body and our soul* – as if they were a single body to cry out to God. The spirit of man is always ready to seek God, and it is like an internal spark inside the human being. The human spirit can make itself feel like that inner consciousness or *hunch* that tells us that is time to look for our Father Creator.

Not so our physical body. Most of the time our flesh is not in its best disposition to seek spirituality. This is because our material body is weak and it feels uncomfortable because it suffers from all kinds of needs. In the same manner, our soul (*personality and mind*) is always thinking of other things, and it is very easy to get distracted by any insignificance or banality.

That we achieve this unity to seek God is indispensable. Because when this union is attained, it is when more supernatural things begin to happen in our lives. Let us look at what is written in the Bible in the following quote:

> *Matthew 15:8. "All of you praise me with your words, but* ***YOU NEVER*** *really* ***THINK ABOUT ME****.*

Here we can see that God complains about there being no unity in the human being to seek for him with **<<all>>** of our being. Reaching this union is extremely important. This is because when a person completes unity with himself to seek God, the individual also realizes a fusion with God himself. As an example of this, we can see that Jesus sought <<unification>> with his Divine Father at all times. The Bible tells us that Christ kept looking for God from very early in the mornings, even before the sun rose.

It is also written that one day, even Jesus fasted for forty days in the wilderness, seeking this same union. Another thing that happens with this matter of unity is that when we become <<one>> with God – *we really step aside*. Because, when we become one with God, he will always be greater and we let him magnify himself in us. Is it not written in John 3:30 that He must increase in importance, while I become less important? This was said by John the Baptist, recognizing that he had to let Jesus take the leadership of the group of Jews who awaited the redemption of the Israelite people. For us Christians, those words take on a very special spiritual meaning.

THE CELESTIAL KINGDOM

Esteemed reader, what you have read so far is to show you that you can see this world in which you live from a different perspective. If after what you have already read you still doubt the existence of Heaven or Hell, I understand, for it is hard for you to believe. Having doubt is not a bad start, because doubt is part of the very nature of a human being.

Nonetheless, I encourage the reader to seek the truth that can only be discovered through – *the desire, the faith, and one's own personal experience*. Therefore, I hope that doubt will not stop you, instead, I long that you will use that doubt to motivate yourself to look for answers. I myself had to experience many supernatural events to be able to believe that there are other dimensions that await the human being after the death of the physical body. The spiritual realm is very willing to interact with the human being. However, just as God wants to have contact with you, Satan also **<<besieges>>** your soul and will seek opportunities to approach you. An individual not believing in heaven does not harm the spiritual world, for that kingdom is permanent. More likely, the person damages himself by not believing in it. If the individual does not have a spiritual life, he will not be as happy as he could be, since the person will always feel as though something is missing. Without the reality of the spiritual realm in our daily existence, human life is lived with a degree of <<uncertainty>> over what will happen tomorrow. But once the person is already a citizen of the Celestial Kingdom, it does not matter if life ends on this world today, since the spiritual individual will already belong to another dimension and to another reality. The person who experiences a spiritual life with Jesus, day after day will feel safer and more confident.

FAREWELL

Remember that you are not being asked to do something that is impossible. No one is demanding that you go up to the moon, or that you go down to the deepest of the seas. Salvation is as close as in your own mouth and in your very own heart. The Bible quotation in the book of Deuteronomy chapter thirty, with lines one to fourteen, will tell you what I just mentioned. To reach God, there are no **<<macabre>>** rites to follow, either. Salvation is relatively easy to attain, and it is free, since you do not have to pay anything to achieve it. Redemption of the soul is an aid and a gift from God to humanity. And with this last biblical quote I say goodbye, trusting that what you have read will show you what you need to do to save your soul, and be happier with the rest of your life.

> *Deuteronomy 30:19. "Today* ***I AM GIVING YOU A CHOICE OF TWO WAYS****. And I ask heaven and earth to be witnesses of your choice. You can choose* ***LIFE OR DEATH****. The first choice will bring a blessing. The other choice will bring a curse. So, choose life! Then you and your children will live.*

Peace and love to all!

REGARDS FROM XAVIER AND THERESA RODRIGUEZ

God bless you dear readers. We wish for this book to be uplifting and to help you scrutinize the scriptures with a fine-toothed comb. This book is a testimony that is real and truthful regarding the great things that God does in our lives and regarding the bonds and chains that we may be carrying for lack of knowledge of the truth. This book also encourages the reader to seek a closer and a more real relationship with God. Our prayer is that this testimony will touch your lives and lead you to a spiritual revival.

Xavier and Theresa Rodriguez

DISCLAIMER

When writing this book, I used the Holy Bible: the contemporary English and easy-to-read versions published in 1995 and 1997, respectively. These have been my favorite Bibles for many years. When comparing Bibles, I chose these versions for its modern language, as they are easy to understand and to communicate about.

Having made this clarification, I will add that there are different biblical translations and that the meaning of some verses could change from one version to another. This happens because the original Bible was written in Aramaic, Greek and Hebrew, and often the grammar and vocabulary of one language are not the same as those of another. A literal translation of those languages to our native tongue would only create a reading that is difficult to understand. The people in charge of creating a biblical translation have always tried to convey the original meaning, while at the same time making sure that the text is easy to read. But, despite the fact that so many bibles exist, someone is always discontent and is always working on a new translation, and that is why there are different biblical versions. Therefore, I make known that the same message this book has given can be found in each different translation, but the quote and verse could change locations.

If it happens that the reader has questions about some of the various spiritual concepts this book has dealt with, I advise that person to scrutinize the sacred biblical texts to confirm the recommendations that have been given in this manuscript.

Now, speaking of another subject, and specifically about the interactions between human beings and the spirits, I can say that I have taken courses in medicine and psychology at the professional and a university level in educational establishments in different countries.

Taking that into account, I acknowledge that not all physical and/or mental ailments, nor all exceptional behaviors a person may exhibit, are caused by satanic entities and/or by demonic possessions.

This can happen because there may exist transient illnesses, mental sufferings, hereditary diseases, and/or systemic diseases in the body of a human being.

These disorders in turn, may very well be the cause of one or more abnormal syndromes in a person.

To the individual who would like to expand his knowledge in this matter, I recommend attending to a doctor, psychologist, psychiatrist, pastor, priest and/or more specialists to assess, compare and/or to rule out symptoms and to proceed with the indicated proper diagnosis and treatments.

Changing again the topic and speaking now of fasting, I can say that for all those people who wish to fast, you should speak with a doctor to inform and educate yourself about the risks and effects that fasting can have on the human body. Consequently – *if it is presumably necessary for the individual* – to take the necessary measures to protect himself, so as not to fall into some sort of ailment.

CONTACT AND INFORMATION

To order online:
http://www.amazon.com

To contact online:
http://www.virgozusa.com

To contact by letter and regular mail:
Virgo Zusa
P.O. Box 530092
San Diego, CA, 91253-0092

www.ingramcontent.com/pod-product-compliance
Lightning Source LLC
Chambersburg PA
CBHW071457040426
42444CB00008B/1385
9780692797563